Peyote

Peyote

A True Account of the Search for the Magic Cactus

by Brian K. Crawford

The Crawford Press
San Anselmo, California

The Crawford Press
72 Oakland Avenue
San Anselmo, California 94960-1614
(415) 454-3439
www.BrianCrawford.info

Contents

Introduction

In January 1968 I was twenty years old and a professional hippie. I traveled around the country living cheap and easy, supporting myself when necessary by buying and selling marijuana and psychedelics. The authorities thought I was a diabolical drug pusher, wrecking the lives of innocent young people for my own profit. But I never pushed anything or anybody. I was just one of a huge number of people who took a lot of recreational drugs. Since they were also illegal, we had to have our own economy and distribution system. So many of us bought more than we used, if we ever had the money and the opportunity at the same time, and resold it. But the money I made just went for groceries and more drugs. I wasn't in it for the money; on the contrary, I was doing it to get rid of money forever. I was a missionary.

It was an exciting time. I was part of a subculture that was changing the world. We were a worldwide nation without borders or laws or government, and our capital was San Francisco. I had spent six weeks there the previous summer, the famous Summer of Love, when food, drugs, and sex were handed out free on the street, and the ocean of love and oneness with each other had pervaded the very air of the Haight. I still carried that feeling within me, and I was intent on spreading it throughout the world.

It was a wonderful, hopeful time for us hippies. We truly thought that we had created a new world order; a world in which war, violence, racism, governments, and working for money all would fade away. And it was a revolution like none other in history - without violence, without speeches and activism and politicking; a revolution created solely by our own living example. And it was psychedelic drugs that had made it all possible.

People tried psychedelics for every kind of reason: some wanted to learn more about themselves; others just wanted a thrill; many just wondered why the governments were all trying to make psychedelics illegal. Timothy Leary was urging everyone to turn on and drop out; the Electric Kool-Aid Acid Test was touring the country passing out acid-laced Kool-Aid from a washtub free to all takers. But whether their motives were sacred or profane, just about everybody who went on a trip came back fundamentally changed. Material possessions and financial success were less important. What mattered was personal relationships, love for the Earth and its inhabitants, and delving ever deeper into the nature of reality with the aid of these marvelous new tools.

It was a heady concept. All through history, reasonable minds have wondered why people can't just stop fighting and live in peace. We had the answer - they hadn't taken acid yet. And we didn't need to form a party and join the political struggle to effect our program. Politics too was irrelevant. All we had to do was to continue living the way we wanted, and everyone would eventually join us. Simply by living in peace and love, without money or jobs, without ownership, guided by the golden rule and our trust and belief in ourselves, we would prove to the world that it could be done.

And the world really was changing - the Prague Spring, the student uprisings in Paris and Berkeley, the anti-war demonstrations drawing millions to the streets of New York and Washington. It was clear the movement was growing. Soon the world would be at peace for the first time since our species arose. The Damocletian sword of nuclear annihilation would be beaten into a peace sign. For young people who had grown up assuming that we would never live to grow up, who were being shoved unwillingly into the meat grinder of Vietnam, it was our hope and our life.

For about a year, from early 1967 until mid-1968, it was possible to believe this dream. Then in one year it was destroyed forever - the assassinations of King and RFK, the burning cities, the crushing of the young people in Prague, in Paris, in Berkeley, in Chicago; the deaths of Jimi Hendrix, Janis Joplin, and Jim Morrison; the arrests of Timothy Leary and Ken Kesey; the ongoing slaughter in Vietnam; and finally the massacre at Kent State, making it all too concise and too clear, as Dylan said, that the world wouldn't tolerate love.

But in January 1968 the dream was fresh and alive.

Chapter One
Boulder

I found myself in Boulder Colorado, and glad of it. It had been a long strange trip across the country from Ohio, and Boulder felt like a safe haven after the redneck horrors of the Great Plains. Boulder is a college town, which always helps liberalize the atmosphere, but it was also a town with a significant hippie population, one of the few way stations on the great underground railroad between the East Village and the Haight-Ashbury. It was a pleasure to see other hippies on the streets again, and to be able to resume trade again.

I was traveling with a girl, Elissa, a college freshman I had met the summer before while peddling LSD on the Champaign-Urbana campus of the University of Illinois. I had walked onto the campus cold and started looking for possible buyers. In those days it was generally safe enough to approach strangers on the street if they looked like hippies, but it was a pretty straight campus and I was nervous. Then I spotted a girl coming out of the student union, her bra-less breasts swaying under a very short Indian print dress, hippie love beads around her neck, a tie-dye headband around long straight brown hair. She was a welcome sight for more reasons than one, and I approached her. She introduced me to her friends and within twenty-four hours I was on my way home with an empty stash, three hundred dollars and a record collection that had been traded to me in desperation for a bag of Vietnamese black, plus fresh memories of a magical night introducing an impressionable young Elissa to the joys of sex in the land of Lysergia.

I was still nominally in school at Antioch College at that time, but by the end of fall quarter I had given up even the pretense of study. I enrolled in what was known as an interim quarter, ostensibly a break to "find myself," but actually a way to avoid being found by my friends and neighbors at the local draft board. At that time every male not exempt was being shipped out to Nam as fast as they could load the planes, and undesirables like blacks and hippie drug-dealers were first in line. With the tacit cooperation of my bleeding heart liberal arts college, I could retain my 1-S student exemption indefinitely.

The sniffing of the draft board, the lure of streets paved with Acapulco gold in San Francisco, and all my natural inclinations combined to cause me to follow Horace Greeley's advice. I went west right after the holidays.

I was traveling light, with only a solid body bass guitar and a beat-up old army duffel bag containing my clothes, three Baroque recorders, and my samples case. I would be traveling hard, but I saw no reason to forego female companionship. I called Elissa and asked if she wanted to go west with me. She packed a bag, snuck out of her father's house in the dead of a cold winter's night, and met me at the bus station. By morning we were long gone into the wastes of Iowa, after having proved that, yes, you can do anything you want in those big back seats of a Greyhound bus at night.

We reached Boulder the following night. At that time there was a thriving hippie street scene going on along Pearl Street in Boulder even in the depths of winter, and soon we were doing good business in grass, hash, and psychedelics. The locals had a lot of psilocybin from Mexico, which had been rare and treasured in Ohio, but they had rarely seen good USP quality Owsley acid, and Elissa and I were welcomed into the bosom of the community.

We found a place to crash in a hippie house on the aptly named Pleasant Street. The other denizens were an interestingly motley bunch from the far reaches of the hippie world, each with great raps about their home scenes. We felt right at home and soon had many friends. When not dealing, we would often hike up into the Rockies that reared abruptly out of the great plains right at the end of our street, and we had many a mystical experience climbing on the snowy Flatirons or exploring abandoned gold mines with our heads full of chemicals.

While we loved Boulder and our friends there, both of us were anxious to push on. The lure of San Francisco was incredibly intense then. It seemed a magical city, beautiful and remote. It was also the source of so much of our music and posters, the art forms that served as the communication channels linking the far-flung colonies of hippies around the world. San Francisco was our Mecca, and we all had to make our pilgrimage. We began passing the word on the street to find us a ride to California, but before anything turned up, a man came to town with a treasure of legendary proportions.

I was in my usual haunt, a corner coffeehouse that commanded a view of the prime dealing territory. A friend named Ollie came in, looked around, and hurried over to me.

"Brian, listen. Have you ever done peyote?"

"No, man, but I've always wanted to. That's the Indian magic cactus, right? It's where mescaline comes from. I keep hearing stories about how righteous it is, but I never met anybody who actually tried it."

"You want some, man?"

"You have some?"

"I can get it."

"Out of sight. How much is it?" I had fears of some exorbitant prices. Even hippie commodities tended to be based on supply and demand, and something as rare and legendary as peyote could command just about any price.

"It's cheap. Five bucks a trip."

"That can't be, man. That's cheaper than plain old acid. Are you sure?"

"Yeah. I met this dude. Never seen him before. He just walked up to me on the street and says, 'Wanna cop some peyote?' Just like that."

"So you get some?"

"Shit, yeah, I bought a hit, but now I've got no more bread. I thought you might get into it. You always go for the exotics."

"Damn right. One book I read said it's at least as strong as acid, but completely natural and organic. It's mainly mescaline, but with dozens of other psychoactive alkaloids in it. The Indians do it, for Chrissake, how much more natural can you get? Where is this dude?"

"Down at the laundromat. Come on."

"My feet have wings."

I was excited as we hurried out into the falling snow. I had always wanted to try peyote. It was one of the few psychedelics I had never tried and I wanted to both see what it was like and if at all possible to add it to my inventory. In my trade it was very important to have both a wide selection and to be as knowledgeable as possible. I had developed a great drug rap, a sort of sales patter full of drug trivia and anecdotes, that knocked the socks off the provincial hippies in places like Boulder. A good drug rap always fascinated the hippie ladies, too. It definitely added to one's coolness factor. Being able to add something as rare as peyote to my repertoire would be a real coup. So I really wanted to meet this guy. I had a bad feeling he would be gone, that this would turn into one of those sad "the one-that-got-away" stories.

In moments we were at the Boulder Laundry (a name that had struck me as hilarious one night on a trip), one of the few free places to get warm on bitter winter days. The guy was still there. I looked him over. He was older than most of us, probably thirty. He was in traditional hippie attire: a fringed buckskin jacket over a paisley shirt and several strings of beads, and bellbottom jeans with lots of holes. But he also wore a very authentic-looking Indian medicine pouch on a thong tied tight around his throat. I was impressed. The guy looked cool. Ollie introduced us in standard dealing protocol, without using names.

"This is the dude I was telling you about, man."

We exchanged the hippie handshake, but he added a funny twist at the end that made me think that he came from places I hadn't been to. I usually felt cool and in charge in my deals, and it made me uncomfortable to think this guy was hipper than I was. He looked me over as well, but I couldn't tell what he thought.

"So you want buttons," he said, immediately putting me at a disadvantage. Drugs were always referred to by their street names when dealing, partly out of discretion and partly to establish oneself as a knowledgeable authority. I collected street names assiduously and I could talk about dope all night without ever calling it the same name twice. But I'd never encountered peyote before and I had never heard any other name for it. Unwilling to admit ignorance, I assumed we were both talking about peyote and ignored the unfamiliar term.

"Yeah. You holding here?" I said, though I was aware of the telltale pause in my reply. Did he know I wouldn't know peyote if I saw it?

"In my wheels." This was a bad sign. He didn't have any peyote to show me, and he wasn't likely to take me to his car. A dealer wouldn't normally take the risk of letting an unknown customer be able to identify his car. It also sounded like the beginning of the old "give me the money and I'll go get it" scam. We were all brother hippies, but I'd been burned on that one before.

"Hey, I don't front, man," I said.

"That's cool. Come on out to the car."

So the three of us buttoned up our coats and went out into the snow. He led us two or three blocks through residential side streets. I was just getting nervous about being led to either a bust or a rip-off when he stopped by a car. It was a Travelall; one of those humongous ugly station wagons put out by International Harvester or somebody. The back and side windows were all painted black. Mud was smeared casually on the license plates to make them illegible, but I could see they were Texas plates. It sure didn't look like a hippie car. My nervousness increased. My bust antenna was twitching. I glanced at the houses around us, half expecting to see a cop camera peeping out from behind a curtain. He led us around to the back and swung open the big back door of the wagon. A musky, earthy odor drifted out into the night air. I stared in astonishment. The entire car was full of brownish green lumps, from the back of the driver's seat to the back door and all the way to the ceiling. Two or three dropped out on the pavement. He bent and tossed them carelessly back in.

"How many you want, man?"

"Jesus," I gasped, all attempts at out-cooling him forgotten. "Where the hell did you get all that?" It was a question one never asked in a drug deal, of course, but he just smiled.

"Well now, that wouldn't be wise for me to spread around, would it? But I'll say one thing, and you can take it from me. I know, cause

I cut 'em myself. These are Roma buttons, and there's none finer in the world."

Roma. I committed that name to memory. If nothing else, it would be an impressive bit of trivia to casually let drop in future raps. Right now I was more interested in the deal. I found I only had sixty bucks on me, so I bought a dozen on the spot. He dug through the pile and pulled out some big ones one at a time and handed them to me.

"I can get more money tonight," I said. "Hell, I can have five hundred by tomorrow."

"No, man, I'm rolling now. This load won't keep much longer. Best to eat 'em fresh. I got to move on. Enjoy. And don't eat the fuzz!"

He drove off into the snow flurries and into drug legend. I looked down at the peyote clutched in my hands. They were unimpressive and unappealing: flat round disks of a consistency like an overripe apple, dark green on top, a sickly yellow-green below. The top was divided into lumpy segments, each with its tuft of dirty white fuzz, and a larger knot of prickly thorns in the center. The bottom surface where it was cut was slimy. All the buttons were smeared with a reddish mud that didn't rub off. They had an unpleasantly rank earthy smell, like that under an old house after a long rainy season.

"What the hell do I do with them?" I asked Ollie.

"Eat 'em. He showed me how to cut the fuzz off. Don't eat that. He says it has strychnine in it. I tried to wash the mud off mine, then closed my eyes and ate it as fast as I could."

"Why fast? Is it stronger that way?"

"No, man. Because it tastes so bad. You won't believe how bad it tastes."

My heart sank. This was the pure magical food of the Indian gods? "It tastes bad? How bad?"

He considered for a few minutes. "Let me put it this way. If it didn't get me to such a beautiful place, I'd rather eat a dog turd than eat another one of those things. And I'm not kidding."

"What? Really? What's it like? The high, I mean, that's enough metaphors on the taste."

"Well, first you feel kind of nauseous from eating the disgusting slimy thing. Then you feel like you're going to get sick."

"But that goes away?" I asked hopefully.

"No. Then you do get sick. I barfed my guts out. But try to keep it down as long as you can so you can get as much of the good stuff out of it as you can. When you have to, let it go. You'll feel a little better, but still sick for a while. Then after a while you realize you're high. Then you realize you're so high it doesn't even matter that you still feel sick. Then you forget all about being sick."

"Christ almighty. You sure it's worth it?"

"Try it. You'll see. I just wish I could afford more."

"Oh here, man. Take these two. You deserve it. Thanks a lot for turning me on to that dude. But I've never been much into nausea as recreation. I hope I still thank you after I eat these lunch launchers."

"You will, brother, trust me."

I hurried back to the crash pad to find Elissa, not without some misgivings. She was there, curled up in a big overstuffed easy chair, reading. The place was quiet except for a couple screwing noisily in one of the bedrooms. A tall skinny kid who always wore a Greek captain's cap and was thus known as Skipper looked up from cleaning a lid of weed on an album cover, carefully rolling the seeds into a film canister. Angel, an Italian kid from New York, and his chick Sunshine (one of about a dozen girls of that name I met during those years) were at the water pipe, bubbling merrily as usual in the center of the room.

I walked in and kicked the snow off my boots. "Hi babe," I said to Elissa, "take a look at this." I went to the old kitchen table and emptied the ten buttons out of my coat pockets. They tumbled soggily to the scarred Formica. Everyone gathered around.

"Yuck," said Elissa, wrinkling her nose. "They're disgusting."

"Guess what these are?" I asked, enjoying the blank stares of all these experienced druggies.

"Petrified elephant snot?" asked Angel.

"They look like the buds of those pod things in *Invasion of the Body Snatchers*," suggested Skipper. "What the hell are they?"

"This, ladies and gentlemen," I said, "is the spirit cactus of the Navajo. The food of the gods of the Anasazi. The key to the gate of the spirit world. Behold... peyote."

"Wow," gasped everyone together. Everyone had heard of peyote, but only as a semi-legendary Indian sacrament, not something slimy on their kitchen table.

"Far out," said Elissa, looking at them dubiously. "Where'd you get them?"

"Some dude passing through town. He's gone already. This is all I could get."

"They smell like they look," said Sunshine, wrinkling her nose.

"No, man, they're supposed to look like that. They're Roma buttons. That's the best in the world, you know."

"Roma? That's a tomato," said Angel.

"Whatever. There they are. Let's do 'em." Since I had revealed my stash in the crash pad, it was rightly assumed that they were to be shared by all.

"What do you do with them?"

"Eat 'em."

"Really?" Everyone stared at them. Skipper reached out and gingerly touched one. He pulled his finger back quickly.

"Shit. They're slimy. They're covered with mud and slime."

"Well, we can wash the mud off. Maybe that'll get the slime off too. And we're supposed to cut all that white shit off. Don't eat that."

"Oh, great. These are sounding better and better."

"It's supposed to be one of the best highs ever."

That did it. The five of us divvied them up. We got a pot of water and we all sat around the table, scrubbing the buttons with a dish washing scrubby. I got out my long evil-looking pocketknife and we dug the fuzz out. The little tufts scraped off, but the central clump went deep and had to be cut out like taking the eyes out of a potato. Worse yet, the fuzz turned out to be microscopic cactus thorns that stuck in our skin and stayed there, hurting invisibly for days afterward. We ended up cutting the buttons into bite size chunks. They were slightly more presentable, but the act of handling and cutting them had greatly intensified their odor. A rank smell filled the room.

"Shit, are they supposed to smell like that or are they rotten?" Elissa gasped. We were all feeling a bit nauseous just from handling and smelling them. No one looked very anxious to put one in his mouth. But I had bought them and I had a rep to maintain as a guy who would try absolutely anything. Besides, it was clear that they were rancid. If we waited they would only go bad and I'd never know what peyote was like.

"Right, then," I said with much more enthusiasm than I felt. I picked up the largest piece, looked at it for a second, and popped it into my mouth. It was even worse than I expected. It had an earthy, gritty nauseating taste, the smell became a hundred times worse when I bit into it, and the texture was like a mealy rotten potato. The combination was hard to handle. Still, I suspected that the more I chewed it the more psychoactives I would extract, so I gamely masticated it into a slimy mess and swallowed it. My stomach immediately let me know it was not enthusiastic for more. Everyone was watching my face. I smiled weakly.

"Not so bad," I mumbled, then decided I should keep my mouth tightly closed for a while. After a few minutes had passed and I kept it down, the others each tried a piece. Their faces paled at the first taste, but we all plowed on, resolutely eating one lump after another until the ten buttons had been forced down five throats. Elissa's normally golden complexion went green, but she bravely continued. We sat back, waiting to see what would happen.

Nothing did for a long time. The couple that had been fucking finally emerged from the bedroom. None of us knew either of them. The girl looked about fifteen.

"God, man, what's that awful smell?" asked the rumpled Lolita, looking around as if she expected to find a long-forgotten corpse in the corner.

"Uh, we just did some peyote," mumbled Skipper.

"Damn, smells like it just did you," said the guy. The two of them hurried out into the cold. We continued to sit staring at each other and trying vainly not to think about throwing up. After a while it was impossible. First Sunshine, then Skipper and Angel struggled to their feet and rushed to the bathroom. The sounds they made in there did not help Elissa and me.

"Try to keep it down if you can," I suggested helpfully, and she certainly did try, but soon she clutched her mouth and ran out. I didn't last much longer, and soon I was also talking to Ralph on the big porcelain telephone. As disgusting as the stuff had been going down, it was much worse coming back. It did give immediate relief to be rid of it however.

I had a big drink of water and washed my face. Feeling slightly better, I returned to the living room. Four large grins met me. Not until then did I realize just how stoned I was.

In those days we were literally always stoned. Grass was a constant, and there was at least one pipe or joint being passed around every hour of the day and night. Hash or opium was sprinkled into the pipe occasionally if we had it. Speed, either in pills called white lightning or as pure Methedrine crystal to be snorted or shot, was common, often leading to several consecutive days of twenty-four hour drugging, uninterrupted by the need for sleep.

Against this background the psychedelics were the main events, lasting from an hour or two with the tryptamines like DMT or DPT, six to eight hours for psilocybin, twelve or so for acid, up to twenty-four or more for STP. Most of these trips were simply recreational - enhancing a rock concert, lovemaking, or a night on a mountaintop; or just enjoying the colorful and fascinating visuals. But a few were intense, soul-changing events. Sudden insights into the nature of reality and the oneness of being would stand revealed with a crystal clarity of self-evident truth. These epiphanies, what Zap Comix called "kosmik trooths," were the things I lived for — to push the envelope, going further and further inward, trying to find at last The Meaning of It All. These experiences gave significance to a lifestyle otherwise merely hedonistic.

Now as I stood looking at my friends there in that crash pad in Boulder, I knew that I was off on another of those voyages of discovery. If you've never tripped, I can't tell you how I knew that or what it felt like. If you have, I don't need to. The visuals were coming on nicely already - pleasant, organic, earth toned. Everything was surrounded with concentric bands of color, as if outlined with several magic markers. Living things, specifically the five of us and a much put-upon communal cat, seemed to pulse with a golden glow from within. There was none of that frenetic jittering, sharp angles, and dayglow colors of LSD, and none of its nervous intensity. I was calm and peaceful and suffused with affection for these dear friends, most of whom I had known less than two months.

Elissa looked especially beautiful; warm and soft and female as she smiled up at me from the ratty old couch covered in an ancient Madras woodblock print. The psychedelic posters on the walls glowed in their usual garish colors, but what appealed now was the gracefully curving letters twining around them. I felt wonderfully content. I found that Ollie had been right. If I thought about it I did still feel sick, but I also felt so good it didn't matter.

After the initial rush was past, we started talking, each trying to tell the others what he was feeling, what was happening to him, but it couldn't be done. We also realized that our feeble attempts to verbalize the experience were distracting us from it. We fell into that strange companionable silence common only to people who get very stoned together frequently. Elissa and I sat side by side, holding hands, and that contact was intense enough to occupy us both for what seemed like hours.

One's sense of time is one of the first casualties of a stoned lifestyle, and hippies rarely wore watches or had clocks. Timepieces were suspect. There was something vaguely fascistic about their measured uniformity. Also, there was nothing like a startled, "Shit, look at the time!" to shatter the fragile shell of timelessness that surrounds a tripper. So none of us had the slightest idea how long it had been since we dropped. Suddenly Skipper groaned and sat up.

"You know, I think I'm getting sicker."

This was both a bringdown and a surprise, since I had been too stoned to think about my stomach for hours. The rest were in my camp, mildly nauseous but not uncomfortable. There didn't seem to be anything to do about it, so we continued contemplating the wonders of the universe. But Skipper seemed to be getting worse by the minute. We all forced ourselves to concentrate on the problem.

"But we all ate about the same amount," said Sunshine.

"And I don't think it's an overdose," I added. "The girls are okay and they had bigger doses by body weight."

"Maybe his stomach is just more sensitive," said Elissa. "That happens."

"Maybe you're just thinking about it too much. Maybe you don't really feel any worse than we do but you're not letting it go."

"Yeah. Think stoned, not sick."

He tried that, but it didn't last. Soon he was holding his belly and groaning. Then he got the dry heaves.

"Hey," I said. "I have a thought. Did everyone cut all the fuzz off the buttons?"

Everyone nodded but Skipper. "I started to, man, but they kept getting stuck in my fingers. I scraped most of them off, but I passed on the middle part."

"Shit, man," I said. "That's it. The fuzz has strychnine in it."

"What?" they all gasped.

"Yeah. Dig it, man. You've been sitting here half the night with strychnine poisoning and you're so stoned you didn't know it."

"Damn, what are we going to do?" We all knew we couldn't go to a hospital. In those days going in with a drug-related emergency meant you were released after treatment straight into jail. Skipper jumped up.

"Well, I gotta do something, man. This shit is killing me." He went to the door. We were all amazed that he could even stand up, much less go out. Before anyone could say anything, he opened the door and immediately disappeared. A tremendous thumping and crashing ensued.

"What the fuck?" said Sunshine, jumping up.

"Shit, the silly bastard fell down the stairs."

We all struggled up and went out onto the landing. There was Skipper, piled up at the bottom of the stairs, looking up at us in surprise. His back had slammed against the door of the downstairs apartment. As we stared, the door opened and Skipper rolled into the apartment and against the legs of a pretty girl in a nightgown. She looked from Skipper to us. I led the rest of us carefully down the stairs.

By the time we got down there she had him stretched out on the floor and was examining his head with assured competence.

"What happened?" Skipped groaned. "Oh, my stomach."

"Is he okay?" Elissa asked.

"I think so," she said over her shoulder. "Nothing's broken anyway."

"Are you a doctor?" asked Sunshine.

"I'm a nurse. I think he'll be okay. He keeps complaining about his abdomen, but I can't find anything wrong." She was checking his ribs and palpating his stomach.

I looked at her. She seemed nice, and any neighbor who had lived under that apartment for very long without complaining to the cops couldn't be all bad. I decided to tell her.

"It's not the fall. It's strychnine poisoning," I said. "He ate peyote and he didn't cut the fuzz off."

"Peyote? No wonder he was so relaxed when he fell. Well, so much for the ER. That's a sure bust. Where the hell did he get peyote? I've never seen it around here." I shrugged.

"How much did he take?"

"Two buttons, about this big around. But he threw them all up a while ago."

"Were they fresh?"

"No. I think about a week old."

"Hmm. That's probably not too dangerous. It loses most of its potency after a few days." She looked at me, then the others.

"Did you all do it?"

I nodded. I still wasn't sure we should be telling her all this, but we had to do what we could for Skipper. She studied me.

"Did you do all of it?"

I nodded again.

"Shit," she said. "Next time score some for me."

We stared at her in amazement, then grinned.

"Well, you guys are too messed up to be much use to him. Leave him here. I'll take care of him."

Heaping thanks on her, we helped lift him onto her couch.

"You okay, Skip?" asked Angel.

"Yeah, I think so. I'll be all right. She's nice, huh?"

"The best, man, the best. We'll see you in the morning."

We trooped back upstairs with relief. We were still flying, but clearly on the way back down. Now we just felt happy. Suddenly Angel laughed.

"Shit, man, can you believe that Skipper? He staggers out of the place poisoned and falls right into a nurse's apartment. And she's a doll. Wow, maybe I should have eaten the fuzz, too."

Sunshine elbowed him for that, but we all laughed together. Now that the scare was over, I thought about the trip we'd just had. There was something about peyote that struck a chord in me. I knew that what I wanted to do now was to find out how to get more peyote.

Chapter Two
The Ambulance

A week or so after that trip Elissa and I gave up on getting a ride to San Francisco and hitched the thirty miles to Denver. We found a fair-sized hippie scene in a rundown neighborhood. We asked around and found a crash pad. It was ratty and Denver didn't appeal to either of us, so we spent most of our time putting up cards in restaurants and on college bulletin boards, trying to find a ride. I did take time to add the Colorado statehouse to my collection of state capitols I had done acid trips in.

We had been there four or five days when a guy Elissa had met came up to us one morning in a coffeehouse where we had taken to hanging out.

"Hey, Elissa," he said. "You still looking for a ride west?"

"Sure," she said.

"Well, there's these people I met who are going to Albuquerque."

"They got room for both of us and our shit?"

"I think so. They're driving an ambulance."

"Well, that should be inconspicuous," I said.

"Yeah, but you'd never get caught in traffic jams," added Elissa. "When do they want to leave?"

"Right now. They were just going to get gas."

"Damn. Where are they?"

"I asked them to stop by here on their way out of town. They said they would. They need someone to help with the gas."

"Far out," I said. "Elissa, stay here and wait for them. I'll go get our shit."

I ran out and jogged the two blocks to the crash. Soon I was galloping awkwardly down the street, the guitar case, my duffel, and

Elissa's old red suitcase flapping in the breeze. When I got back to the restaurant there was an ancient Cadillac ambulance parked in front. Elissa was talking to a tall man with a heavy black beard and a thin blonde woman in a moth-eaten fur coat.

"Babe, this is Sean and Chris," said Elissa as I puffed up. "This is my man Brian."

"Hi," I said with my best ingratiating smile. I wanted to get out of Denver and the cold.

Sean looked at me without a hint of a smile. "You got money for gas?"

"Some. Not all of it."

"There's two more coming. We don't have no bread ourselves."

"So it'd be split four ways?" I looked at the car dubiously. It was rounded and curvy in what once was called futuristic streamlining, but now just looked funky. One window was cracked and taped together. The paint had faded to a blotchy flamingo pink. The car was obscenely long, with a hood that went out forever.

"What kind of mileage do you get? Will it make it?"

"It'll make it, man. I keep it running good and I got my own tools. It's a '47, with an inline eight. I guess it gets about ten."

"Ten miles a gallon?"

"Ten to twelve," said Chris.

I calculated rapidly. Elissa had no money of her own, so it would be split between the other two passengers and me. It could be a thousand miles to LA, at 50 cents a gallon for the cheap gas, came to maybe fifteen to twenty bucks apiece. I had around fifty from selling out my stock in Boulder. I only had my sample case left. Close, but we could make it.

"We can do that," I said.

"Right. In the back," said Sean, and he and Chris went and got in the front. I opened the back door, one of those big wide mothers that swings around and almost pulls you over. The back of the ambulance was a jumble of bags - duffel, sleeping, and garbage, mixed with an assortment of winter coats and other unidentifiable items. I threw our stuff in along one side, we climbed in, and I reached out and pulled the door shut. The car swerved out into traffic before I could sit down, and I tumbled across the piles of stuff.

"Ow! Hey, shit, man!" came a muffled voice, and a gaunt, hairless figure sat up in the half-light. Elissa let out a squeak, and I tried to crawl back to her where she sat against the back door.

"Fer Chrissake!" said a woman's voice, and the pile shifted under me again.

I crawled on and flopped back beside Elissa. A very pretty blonde head emerged from under a pile of coats.

"Sorry," I said. "I didn't know you guys were under there."

"Well, we spent the night in here and it's colder than a teacher's wit out there." She sat up and the coats fell from her. I gulped. She was naked, and she seemed unconcerned that I was staring at her as she dug a brush out of somewhere and started brushing her hair. I could feel Elissa watching me in disapproval, but I had to stare. She was really a lovely girl about my own age, with long shining blonde hair and absolutely perfect breasts, her nipples stiff in the cold air.

"Uh, I'm Brian, and this is Elissa," I stammered.

"I'm Sara," she said, not glancing toward Elissa. "I don't know his name."

I had forgotten the other resident of the car. I peered forward to where he sat, as straight and motionless as a statue. A head that seemed to be clean-shaven emphasized the likeness to a mannequin. He was thin and wiry, with a lined face and dark eyes a lot older than the rest of him.

"Mike," he said.

"Hi," I replied, then we all settled into silence while the ambulance worked its way out of Denver. I wiped the frost from one window and peered out.

"Hey," I said. "That sign said I-25 south. I thought we were going west."

"Sean said they were going south through New Mexico and Arizona," said Sara. "Stay out of the snow."

"Suits me," I said. "I'm tired of the cold. Aren't you, babe?" Elissa nodded.

"I like the cold," said Mike. That killed the conversation again. This could prove to be a long trip. Mike seemed strange, maybe even hostile, and both of them clearly made Elissa uncomfortable. But I sure liked looking at Sara, though she had snuggled down into the blankets again. But we had many days to spend cooped up with these people and I was determined not to ride in silence.

"So, how long have you known Sean and Chris?" I asked Sara.

"Just met them yesterday. I dumped my old man in Laramie and wanted to go to Santa Fe to see if I could find an old friend. They had a car. They picked Mike up at the same time."

"How about you, Mike?" I was much more interested in talking to Sara, but I thought I better keep up an appearance of equal socializing. "Why are you going to Albuquerque?"

He shrugged. "I just wanted to go somewhere else."

"So, are you and Sara traveling together?"

"No, we're not," said Sara pointedly, looking at me. I tried to read her eyes. Was it just my pornographic fantasy, or was she actually coming on to me? At any rate, with all of us in the back of an ambulance for the next few days it seemed a moot point.

We rolled through southern Colorado, stopping fairly frequently for gas and pit stops. We ate candy bars and cold burritos out of the vending machines in the truck stops. The truckers stared at us when we came in, but they were too busy looking at Sara to take the trouble to harass a bunch of hippies. When we stopped she always pulled on a beaded Indian dress that was so short it barely covered her ass. Knowing as I did that she was naked underneath, I always gulped when she bent over to get the candy out of the vending machine. I couldn't help wondering if she was doing it for the truckers, for me, or if she was even aware of it. She just seemed totally unconcerned about her body. As soon as we were back in the car, she took the dress off and crawled under the blankets. Elissa disliked her for some reason. Mike seemed totally unaware of her. I was fascinated.

Sean and Chris rarely spoke with the rest of us. There was only a small window communicating between the front of the ambulance and the back, and they kept it closed. We'd knock on it if we needed to stop. They kept to themselves even at the stops. They seemed to think of us only as cargo to pay for the trip.

Sean drove long into the night. Then the car slowed and turned off the highway onto a dirt road. We bounced around in the back for a few hundred yards, then the car stopped. Sean slid the window back.

"We're stopping here for the night. I'm too tired to drive any more."

We were all anxious to get on with the trip, and particularly to get out of the snow country. Both Mike and I volunteered to help with the driving, but Sean refused without explanation. He and Chris got out, locked the doors of the cab, and got in the back with us. There was plenty of room, even for six people. We passed around a pipe and got stoned, and fell into the usual getting-stoned-together-for-the-first-time rap.

Elissa and I briefly told our stories. Sara had been living with a guy on a commune in Wyoming, but he was a jerk and she left. She wanted to go to Santa Fe because she'd heard an old flame of hers was living there. Sean and Chris were from Chicago, stone broke, and wanted to go to Albuquerque to check out the scene there. Mike just listened in silence until every one else had told their story.

"What about you, Mike?" Elissa asked. "Where are you from?"

"I'm from LA," he said after a long pause. "I was into the scene there on Sunset Strip, getting high a lot. Then I got drafted. I was afraid to go to jail or to try running to Canada or something, so I thought I'd go get it over with. So they sent me to Nam."

"Wow. You were in Vietnam?" I asked. Lots of my friends had been sent over, but I'd never heard from them again. If they'd come back I hadn't heard about it. It was as if they'd left the Earth. This guy had actually been there and come back. "What was it like?"

"Shitty. The brass are sending units into places where they know they're gonna take heavy hits."

"On purpose?" asked Sara. "Why?"

"Because Johnson wants to get a lot of American kids killed."

"Oh, come on, why would he want that?"

"Two reasons. First, it's a great way to get rid of his enemies. Who really hates Johnson? Kids, blacks, and hippies, right? So who do they send to Nam? Who doesn't come back? Think about it. He can't have us hanged or transported to Australia like the Brits did to keep their dissidents down. And who's to complain? They weren't executed; they were heroes sacrificing for their country. Shit. You don't have to draft heroes. It's a simple choice: two years taking your chances with Charlie, or ten years certain in Leavenworth."

"You said there were two reasons," I said, after we all thought about that for a while.

"Johnson wants the war to escalate. He wants all of Southeast Asia to go up in flames, with lots of GI's killed, civilian atrocities, genocide. Then Johnson's really in business. He can go crazy, sending in armies here, carpet bombing there, and assassination units to capitals. The CIA gets permanent work, the Army is fully geared up, and American arms merchants are making a killing, so to speak. And Congress authorizes any appropriation he requests, no questions asked, no oversight committees. After all, it's a national emergency. Security is at stake."

"Damn," muttered Sean. "Is that what it's really all about?"

"Shit, yeah. Only now some of us who did somehow survive are coming back, telling their friends what they know. People are starting to say, "Hey, Lyndon. Explain again the part about why we're supporting a puppet dictator who's killing and ripping off his own people to stop a free election, just because the people might elect a communist? How many people do you know who have really been worried about Vietnam attacking California? I mean, for most wars they at least tried to come up with an excuse why we should fear and hate the enemy. Now they don't bother."

"Wow. Did you do your whole two years?"

"No, man. I knew I'd never survive that many patrols. They have it figured. The odds are one in twenty that a guy won't come back from any particular mission. So they send you on fifty, just to be sure. I knew one guy who went on sixty-three before he got killed. We called him 'Lucky.'"

"How did you get out?"

"I got a section eight."

"What's that?" asked Sara.

"I was so crazy the army didn't want me."

"Wow, that's really crazy," I said. "I thought it was almost impossible to get out that way."

"It is. I got pretty extreme there."

"What'd you do?"

"Suffice it to say I finally convinced them."

"Did you actually fight the Viet Cong?"

"Hell, yes. I went out on twenty-three patrols."

"Did you see anybody get killed?" asked Elissa. It was hard to believe that this guy our own age was actually a combat veteran. Veterans were big fat old guys in loud suits who hung out at the VFW bars.

"Yeah. Plenty of Charlie and too damn many of my buddies. Let's talk about something else."

"Yeah, this shit is too heavy," said Sean. "Speaking of heavy shit, whose hash is this we're smoking? I'm fucked up."

"Mine," I said. "It's Lebanese brown. Know how they make it? When the dope is in flower, these young Lebanese girls run naked through the fields and they scrape the pollen from their skin."

"What?" said Chris. "Is that really how they make it?"

"I haven't a clue. But somebody told me that once. If it's not true, it should be. Its appeal goes beyond mere truth and it's sold many a block of hash."

"Good shit," everyone agreed. I was pleased my rep for always having the best was sustained.

"Hey, guys," I said. "Elissa and I just got into something great in Boulder. Anybody ever do any peyote?"

"Yeah," said Mike enthusiastically. "I just got some a week ago in Denver. Wild, wild, trip." The others had never done any, but when Elissa and Mike and I raved about our trips long enough they were anxious to try some.

"Where did you get it?" asked Chris.

"Some dude came through town in a big station wagon stuffed to the top with buttons. He was heading out of town when I scored, so I couldn't get any more."

"Hey, that's the same guy I got it from," said Mike. "We tripped together. Did you ever see anything like that car? There must have been ten thousand buttons in it."

"I guessed twenty-five thousand," I said.

"Wow. At five dollars a pop," said Chris in awe.

"I wonder where he got them?" asked Sean.

"I don't know," I answered. "He wouldn't tell me anything."

"Well, he talked a lot when we tripped together," said Mike. "He told me all about how he found them and picked them. He said he followed a line of high-tension wires west out of a town, over three ridges, and then the ground was covered with buttons. He just cut 'em off right at ground level. But he wouldn't tell me anything about where it was."

"Is that right?" I asked. "All he told me was that they were Roma buttons. Could that be the name of the town?"

"Hey, could be," said Sean excitedly. "I wonder what state it's in?"

"It sounds Spanish," Chris suggested. "It could even be in Mexico."

"I don't think so," said Mike. "Can you imagine crossing the border with a car wedged full of buttons? Not too smart."

"He had Texas plates," I suddenly remembered.

"Far out!" shouted Sean. He went and got a Texas road map out of the cab. We gathered around him as he spread it out. Elissa hurriedly scanned the index of towns. She let out a squeak.

"Here it is! Roma, Y7!"

"Man, that's way down here," said Sara. "Let's see, Y... 7!"

"There it is," said Chris, pointing.

"Damn, it's right on the Rio Grande," I said. "That looks like some empty country."

"All the better," said Sean. "Listen, are you guys thinking what I'm thinking?"

"If we know the town and we know how to find them from the town?" I asked. "How can we miss?"

"Hey, there could be big money in this," said Sean. "We could fill this old ambulance to the gills."

"Yeah, man," said Mike. "We could get all the peyote we want and we could all be rich, too."

"Right on!" said Sean. "Who's for going down to Roma?"

"I don't know," said Sara. "That's a long way out of our way. It'd take a week at least, maybe more. I really wanted to get to Santa Fe."

Elissa said she was afraid to go to Texas. It was definitely deep in redneck country, the kind of place hippies avoided. There were rumors of longhairs disappearing down there. But everyone else was for it.

"Look," I said. "Peyote grows in the desert and we'll be going through a lot of desert. Maybe we don't have to go all the way to Roma. How about if we look for it on the way south? If we find it we'll pick a load and take it to LA. If not, we'll go down to Roma and see what we can find."

Everyone agreed to this, and we gradually faded. Sean blew out the candle. We all made nests for ourselves and snuggled down into the dozens of sleeping bags, luggage, and blankets that covered the floor of the ambulance. We were all naked, and it felt good when Elissa curled up in my arms. But I had trouble sleeping because I could feel Sara's bare bottom pressed against mine.

Chapter Three
Sara

It was a long cold night and we were all anxious to get going, so as soon as we were awake Sean and Chris moved back to the cab and we were off at first light. Some of us had heard of a hippie commune in southern Colorado at a place called Trinidad, and we planned to stop in there to see if they knew if peyote grew around there. But when we got to Trinidad none of the locals knew, or would tell us, where the commune was. We decided to spend a few hours walking around in the desert to see if we could find any.

The snow was gone now, but it was still cold. Sean turned off on a dirt road and we bounced along until we were out of sight from the main road. Then we all wandered off looking under bushes for the little green bumps of peyote sticking out of the sand. Elissa and I started following a dry wash, but after a few hundred yards with no luck I climbed out of the wash and started combing the plateau. Elissa continued up the wash, poking along with a stick.

A little later I noticed motion out of the corner of my eye and saw Sara a little distance away, kicking over stones. I moved toward her and she soon looked up and saw me. She waved and dropped down into an intervening wash. I headed that way too.

When I scrambled down the steep bank to join her, she came over to me with a big grin on her face. I thought maybe she'd found peyote.

"Hi," she said.

"Hi."

"I was hoping to get you alone," she smiled.

My heart jumped. So my imaginings hadn't just been wishful thinking. But what could we do here? It was bitter cold and windy, and the ground was all little sharp rocks covered with broken twigs and thorns. I looked around, then turned and shrugged at her.

She knew exactly what she wanted. She pulled me to her and turned, pressing her back against me. She opened the sides of her poncho. Beneath it she wore that short Indian dress. She took my hand, slipped it under her dress, and put it between her legs.

I was taken completely by surprise. It was like holding a small warm furry animal cupped in my icy hand. She put my other hand flat on her belly, then slid it up under her dress to her breast. I thought I was going to explode, but I still couldn't figure out how we were going to do anything.

She started moving my hands on her, and I realized she just wanted me to stroke her. That was fine with me. We stood there in that frigid Colorado high desert wind with her poncho flapping around us, and I used every technique I knew to make it good for her. Soon she was coming, gasping and pressing herself back against me as my hands worked frantically on her body. When she was through, she twisted her head around and gave me a passionate kiss. I let go of her and she buttoned her poncho. We both went back to hunting for peyote, though I was walking with a decided limp. Soon after that I came upon Elissa and Chris. I saw Elissa eyeing Sara when she saw the two of us together.

"Anything?"

"No. Maybe it's too cold here."

"It's too cold for me," said Sara. "Let's go further south."

We rounded up the others and headed for New Mexico. My thoughts were whirling as I lay between Elissa and Sara. We passed around another joint to get warm.

We crossed into New Mexico and the landscape gradually changed. Soon we were in high mountains with lots of pines. We arrived in Taos in mid-afternoon after another night in the car. Taos did have a hippie community and we spent a day there nosing about checking out the scene. None of the local hippies knew of any peyote in the area. They said that the Navajo were known to use it, but they didn't know where they got it.

Disappointed again, we headed toward Santa Fe. As we left town we spotted three teen-age Navajo girls walking along the road laughing. Sean pulled up beside them and rolled down his window. He had a dark threatening look with his full black beard, and the girls drew back. One, however, gave a friendly smile and came over when he beckoned her.

"Yes?" she said, "Can I help you?"

"Yeah," said Sean. "Know where we can get some peyote around here?"

It was exactly as if he had slapped her. Her smile disappeared, her face darkened, and tears came to her eyes.

"No! Get out of here! Go away!" she shouted, and the three of them ran away as fast as they could go.

"Well, shit," said Sean. "No need to get so damn huffy. She could have just said no."

"Hell, man," said Chris. "It's a sacrament for them. It's probably like a dude coming up to some Catholic kids and asking if they knew where he could go to fuck the Virgin Mary or something."

We drove on, but the look on that girl's face has always stuck with me. I felt so sorry for having hurt her that I've always wanted to go back and apologize. So much for consideration of another culture's values. But we continued looking for Virgin Mary.

The thing with Sara was driving me crazy. I still liked Elissa a lot and we were great together, but the memory of that strange trip out on the desert was always in my mind. And it didn't help that Sara was always bouncing around naked in the car. I was so hot and frustrated I thought I would jump her any minute.

I think Elissa was very aware of the heat between us. She snuggled up possessively against me as we bounced along. That last evening before Santa Fe, she began to stroke me under the blankets. I never knew if it was simple lust or if she wanted to prove to Sara that I was her man, but she soon had me more than ready. She was being fairly discrete, but it was perfectly obvious what was going on under the blanket. Then she slipped her head under the blanket and a moment later I felt her mouth on me. I closed my eyes in pleasure. When I opened them, both Mike and Sara were watching my face;

Mike with amusement, and I couldn't be sure what I saw in Sara's eyes. Then as I watched, Sara shifted over beside me. She threw the blankets off herself and again pressed my hand between her legs. Then she slid up a few inches and pressed her breast into my mouth. Mike's mouth dropped open.

It was the strangest sensation, and it didn't help to have Mike watching. No one said anything as the pace accelerated. As one might imagine, it didn't take long. Sara and I came together as Elissa's head bobbed furiously up and down under the blankets, then finally stopped. Sara kissed me and shifted away back under the blankets. A few minutes later Elissa came up for air, a pleased, contented look on her face. She never glanced at Sara, but I'm sure she thought she had put the hussy in her place. She never found out what went on that night.

The next day we reached Santa Fe. Sara's deal was that she had the address of an old lover there, but she wasn't sure he was still there, unattached, or interested, or if she was still interested in him. She wanted to look him up, check out the feelings, and make up her mind then. If it were cool, she'd stay with him. If not, she'd continue with us. I desperately hoped she'd find he'd joined a monastic order. Although I'd had sex with her twice already, I'd never really made love to her, and I was terribly frustrated and hot for her.

We cruised for hours finding the address, a rundown adobe on a back street. She went to the door, a guy came out. They talked for a few minutes, then she came back to the car.

"It's okay," she said. "Can you pass me my stuff?"

I handed it through the window. She said goodbye to everybody, then she went into the house and closed the door. Elissa, and perhaps Mike, breathed a sigh of relief. I never saw Sara again, outside of erotic dreams.

Chapter Four
Big Bend

The rest of us went to a restaurant to plan our next move. We'd talked to a number of hippies in Santa Fe. Some of them had done peyote, but they were sure it wasn't local. The consensus was that all peyote in the states came from either Texas or Mexico. So it appeared that we'd have to go to Texas, though there was still hope we'd find some before we got all the way to Roma. Two of our contacts had mentioned Big Bend State Park as a possible source. Elissa was still dubious. She'd signed on to go to San Francisco with me. This was the wrong direction and sounded too scary for her. But the rest of us all wanted to give Texas a shot and she wanted to stay with me, so in the morning we were on our way east.

It was a long drive to El Paso and further to the turnoff south to Big Bend. We drove several more hours before we came to the ranger station at the entrance. We picked up a map and some camping supplies, then headed on. The road from the entrance gate to the river must be fifty miles of the flattest, loneliest desert any of us had ever seen. We couldn't believe we had gone so far and still hadn't gotten to the river.

At last we came to a dirt road that led to the camping area we had picked out on the map as the most remote. Yet more hours of bumping, this time on a rutted gravel road, then we came out on the edge of a steep valley and saw a line of green trees far below us. It was nearly dark by the time we pulled up on a small beach on the bank of the Rio Grande. We all got out to check it out.

The river at that point was unimpressive, perhaps fifty yards wide but nowhere more than a foot deep. A wagon track went across it, disappearing into the low rolling hills of Mexico on the other side.

Mexico! Land of great marijuana and lax enforcement, of Michoacan green and Acapulco gold and the legendary Sinsemilla - lovely names that rolled off the tongue.

"Shit, man," said Sean. "Why does everybody try to mule it across in California? Nothing could be easier than bringing it across right here."

Mike looked at the map. "There's a little town on the other side, San Vincente. Looks like it's only a mile or two from here."

"Far out. Let's go over there tomorrow and see if we can set something up. If they don't have any shit we can have it trucked in there. What a setup. That ranger didn't give us a second look."

"It can't be that easy, can it?" I asked. "Let me see that map."

Mike passed it over. "Yeah, there's a town over there," I said, "but there's no roads to it. None at all."

"Bullshit. You can't have a town without any roads. How would people get there?"

"Look at the map. This wagon track is the only way in. It's two hundred miles of desert mountains between here and the next town."

"Far out, man," said Elissa. "What a neat place. Let's do go see it tomorrow."

"Maybe they know where the peyote grows," added Chris.

We built a fire, fixed a quick meal, had a companionable smoke, and turned in. The stars burned down out of a sky clearer and darker than any of us had ever seen. We heard coyotes howling during the night.

In the morning we filled some water bottles and splashed across the river to Mexico. We followed the wagon ruts for an hour or so, then could see houses up ahead. There were five of them, all identical small adobes with corrugated iron roofs. They were arranged haphazardly; two facing each other, the others facing out toward the desert stretching away to the horizon in all directions. There were no trees. There was no store or post office, no church, not even a square or main street. The wagon track went between two of the houses, circled around one, and doubled back on itself.

We trudged up to the turnaround before anyone appeared. Then an old man came out of one of the houses and stood looking at us. Mike knew a few words of Spanish so he walked towards the man.

"Hola," he called out when they were twenty-five yards apart.

The man continued to stare.

"Buenos Dias," Mike tried again at five yards.

The man nodded. Mike went up and shook his hand; then they carried on a long painfully slow conversation with much gesturing and sign language. After a while Mike beckoned us over.

"He says they get everything on the wagon from the US side. He doesn't know what peyote is. He has horses we could rent if we want to look around."

"I don't know, man," I said. "That can be expensive. I've been riding a few times and it always cost six or eight bucks an hour."

Mike and the old man talked some more.

"He says a dollar a day per horse."

"Shit, let's do it," I said. "We could cover lots more territory on horses."

"Hey, me and Chris, we've never ridden," said Sean.

"Me either," added Elissa.

"Hey, it's easy. We'll just go slow and walk around looking for buttons."

So we struck the deal. The old man said he couldn't have the horses ready before tomorrow, so we asked him to bring them down to the river early the next morning. We walked back to camp.

We spent a very pleasant afternoon wandering around under the cottonwood trees and playing in the river. We each made several forays into the desert on the US side, but no one saw any peyote. We fixed a good dinner for a change and slept under the stars again.

The next morning at dawn we heard the neighing of horses and got up to see the old man and a boy leading four horses down the bank. We went over to meet them.

"He says they couldn't find the other horse," Mike explained after a short talk.

"That's okay," said Elissa. "I'll ride with Brian."

We paid the man four dollars and he and the boy turned back to the village. We led the horses across the river to camp, had breakfast, packed a lunch, and then mounted up, not without some amusing scenes. Finally we set off west, up the middle of the river.

Since I had had two pony rides as a child and was therefore the experienced horseman, I led the way. The horses were trudging along through the water, no faster than we could have walked. I kept shaking the reins and shouting Giddy up, but nothing happened.

"Hey," yelled Mike. "I know. These are Mexican horses. They don't understand English."

"That's silly," I said. "Giddy up isn't English, it's horse. All horses understand Giddy Up." But just then Mike yelled "Andale! Andale!" and all three horses broke into a run.

We flew up the river, water flying up above our heads, forming rainbows before us in the clear morning air. Everyone was shouting, either in delight or terror, and my heart was pounding. I suddenly realized that it could be dangerous for the horses to run like this where they couldn't see the footing, and I managed to get mine stopped. The others dropped back to a walk as they caught up.

After a mile or so in the river we found a dry wash coming in from the south and went up that until we climbed onto the plateau above the river. We went along slowly, looking for the peyote, but we had found none by the time we stopped for lunch on a high hill overlooking the river. As we munched our apples and trail mix, Mike pointed up the river.

"Hey, what's that big yellow cloud?"

Sure enough, a big bank of what looked like sulfur-yellow fog was heading down the river some miles from us.

"Could it be a rain storm?" asked Chris.

"I don't know. Sure looks funny. It's following the course of the river. Wonder what it could be?"

After lunch we doubled back toward camp. We came out on a bluff towering above the river. The yellow cloud was directly below us, moving down the river. The slope was steep and covered with mesquite and cholla. I started toward the edge, but my horse balked and refused to step over the edge. The others refused as well. We must have spent an hour trying fruitlessly to get the horses started down that slope. I've heard since that horses won't go down a steep slope with an inexperienced rider because they can't see their footing without risking a somersault.

In the end we dismounted and led them down, zigzagging back and forth across the slope. As we went down the wind kept increasing. Soon it was blowing like hell, driving sand into our faces. We realized the yellow fog was a dust storm. By the time we got down it was nearly dark and we still had a mile or more to go in the river, right into the teeth of the sandstorm. It was well after dark that we finally straggled into camp and climbed down thankfully from the horses. We tethered them in some long grass under the cottonwoods and set about making dinner.

We opened the car to get dinner out and found that someone had left one window open a quarter inch to keep the car from getting too hot. The dust storm had deposited a three-inch layer of sand on everything in the car. All hands fell to dragging everything out and flinging the sand into each other's eyes. We never did succeed in getting all of it out of the sleeping bags. Elissa tried to shake out a blanket and the wind dragged her thirty feet before she let go.

We'd bought tortillas and canned refried beans, so we broke out a big cast iron frying pan Chris had and tried to light a fire. It took at least an hour. We had to build a windbreak by piling up river rocks and driftwood upwind of the fire. All nonessential personnel were stationed to windward to try to break the wind. We must have used two boxes of matches before we got the fire lit. Fortunately even impoverished hippies always have plenty of matches.

Finally the fire was going well, but the flames were whipped out flat along the ground for ten or fifteen feet downwind. The only solution was to go down there to set up the frying pan. With the pan resting on some rocks, the flames flickered all around it with a noise like a blast furnace. We put a deep layer of oil in the pan and tried to deep-fry the tortillas. Several times the oil caught fire, and occasionally we'd use the spatula to shovel off the sand that tended to bury the tortilla before it could cook. Those were memorable burritos, but we were so hungry even the spoonfuls of sand in each one didn't stop us.

We had a wild and uncomfortable night in the ambulance as it rocked and rolled in the wind. The storm died during the night and we piled out in the morning to a clear sky. The Mexicans reclaimed their horses, said they hadn't had the dust storm in San Vincente, and left. We'd had enough. We packed up and headed out.

The car was a mess. It had been bad enough when we started, but a lot of unwashed hippies, moldy sleeping bags, and hundreds of potato chip and Frito bags had made it truly rank. Now everything was covered in sand. We decided to splurge and get a motel room.

We found a little place in Alpine just outside the park and the rest of us laid low while Sean rented a single room. He backed the ambulance up right to the door and we unloaded everything. The girls washed clothes in the tub while the guys shook out the bags, blankets, and clothes. The old mattress that we discovered in the bottom of the pile was too disgusting to try to save, so we squeezed it out through the back window of the room and left it. We shoveled and swept out the back of the car and put everything back in. We all had showers, leaving dunes in the tub. Then we all squeezed into the one double bed and slept like logs. We were out before the sunrise and the proprietor could catch us.

Chapter Five
Roma

It took another entire day of driving before we reached the border town of Eagle Pass. It was a scary, redneck-looking place, with rusted-out pickups on blocks in front of ratty little frame houses with peeling paint. We thought it would be fun to cross the border into Piedras Negras, but the American border authorities suggested we get out of town instead. We continued southeast, paralleling the river, to the next border crossing at Laredo to try again.

Since the car was even more conspicuous than we were, we parked it a few blocks away and walked across the bridge. This time the Americans only eyed us with suspicion, and we went through the Mexican customs with only routine questions. Feeling pleased with ourselves, we strolled into the bustling market area of Nuevo Laredo. We wandered along, peering into the shops, soaking up the experience of being out of the U.S. It felt comfortable to be there. We were brothers with these people - both hippies and Mexicans were being oppressed by the Norte Americano military-industrial dictatorship.

We had gone about a block and a half when we heard a commotion behind us. Everyone on the street turned to look back toward the bridge. A half dozen brown-shirted Federales were running down the street, shouting and waving their weapons. We moved up against the shop windows to let them go past us, no doubt in pursuit of some felons. To our amazement, they stopped and started shouting at us. We couldn't understand what was going on, but they hustled us all back to the bridge and made it more than clear that we were not welcome in Mexico now or in any conceivable future administration.

Disappointed and a little hurt by this hostile treatment by our brothers to the south (after all, we were dedicated consumers of

Mexican produce), we trudged back across the long rusty bridge. We assumed the American authorities had called the Mexicans and pressured them to expel us. As we entered the U.S. Customs building for the second time in five minutes, an officer looked up at us.

"How long have you been in Mexico?"

"What?" said Sean. "You just waved us through."

"How long have you been out of the US?"

Sean took a breath to shout, but Chris wisely shushed him.

"Five minutes, officer," she said in her sweetest voice.

"Where did you go in Mexico?"

"About a hundred yards."

"Do you have anything to declare?"

"We didn't have enough time to pick up so much as a coating of dust." Her nice girl tone was wearing thin. The rest of us stood there uncomfortably shuffling our feet.

"Passports, please."

"We don't need passports. We're American citizens visiting Mexico. We just walked across."

"How do we know that, ma'am?"

"You stared at my ass all the way across the bridge, officer. Surely you would remember that?"

He glared at us, then went into a glass-fronted office to talk to another La Migra official. I was afraid they were going to lock us up for not having passports. After all, how could we prove we were American? As far as I knew, none of us had passports. But after a few minutes, the first bozo returned.

"All right. Get out of here. Get out of town and keep going. And don't try to cross into Mexico again, anywhere. Understand?"

"Yeah," Chris sighed. "God, it's nice to be back in a free country again."

We beat it out of there and continued down river. We resolved to skip the tourist sights from now on. We'd go straight to Roma, load up, and get the hell out of Texas.

All the distances are long in Texas, especially for hippies. It's damned hard to be inconspicuous when you've got hair down to your waist, the girls aren't wearing bras, and you're riding in a 1947 red

Cadillac ambulance. We bought food at small gas stations and avoided stopping in towns at all. Finally we came to the outskirts of Roma. Sean slowed down, and for the first time in the trip we came within twenty MPH of the legal speed limit.

Then we crested a ridge and Sean let out a whoop. A long row of tall high-tension towers strode away across the hills like a column of skeletal giants. They ran west from the town over a series of ridges, exactly as the peyote man had said. Sean pulled off the road where a gated dirt track wound off toward the nearest tower. We all stared at that dusty track as if it were paved in yellow bricks.

"This is it, this is it," Mike kept saying. There could be little doubt that this was the place. We grinned at each other. I was relieved and elated to have our detection work prove out - I had been worried that this was the wrong Roma and this whole endless side trip would have been a waste of time. But I was also afraid.

Back in Colorado the idea of driving down here and picking up a load of buttons had sounded so simple. It was a challenge, a puzzle to solve, an adventure. But now here we were in the desert, alone in an alien land. The harsh, uninviting terrain, the rusty barbed wire fences and dilapidated, abandoned ranch houses were grittily real. And the hostile reception everywhere we went had put a somber, threatening tone to the trip.

We felt like resistance fighters in occupied territory. If captured we knew we could expect no mercy. This wasn't an amusing anecdote to some day add to my drug rap. These rednecks were frighteningly real. Every pickup we passed had a rifle rack in the window. The desert looked cold and indifferent. It was all too easy to imagine getting killed out there in that chaparral. A volley of shots, some screams, then silence. We'd never be found out here. I remembered seeing pictures of the shot-up car of three freedom riders murdered by rednecks somewhere out in the South.

On the other hand, about a hundred thousand dollars worth of great highs was lying on the ground within a mile of us right now. We'd come this far; I sure as hell didn't intend to leave without giving it a try. But it was nearly dark, clearly too late to wander off into the desert. We talked about it for a while and decided to spend the night as usual, parked on some old dirt road out of sight of the highway. This one was gated and locked and too close to the peyote. In the morning we'd come back here, get out there and pick until dark, then get the hell out of Texas as fast as we could.

We were all excited, anxious to get started and chafing at having to spend the night. Above all, we were elated at having found the source. Things seemed to be going right for us at last. Then we made a truly disastrous decision.

"Hey," said Sean. "Tomorrow we'll be rich and out of here. We need to celebrate. Know what we should do? Let's go into town and have a good meal in a real restaurant."

Elissa and I both thought it was too risky to go openly into Roma.

"Are you crazy, man?" I asked. "A carload of hippies just happens to stop in for dinner in the peyote capital of America? You don't think they'll put five and a hundred thousand together? Why don't we just have T-shirts made up that say 'Great Peyote Hunt of 1968'"?

"Yeah," added Elissa. "With 'Bust Me' on the back." But everyone else was for it.

"Shit, you guys act like we're knocking over Fort Knox or something," said Chris. "These are simple ranch people. They don't know they're living in peyote heaven. They probably don't know what peyote is. If a cow can't eat it, they don't need to know about it."

"Yeah," agreed Mike. "They'll stare at us, sure, but as far as they know we're just a bunch of freaks passing through. They have no reason to suspect us of anything."

"Besides," put in Sean. "It's not like we're stealing anything from anybody. The cactus isn't doing anybody here any good. It has no value to them. We'll just come out here in the morning and be out of here before dark and no one will be the wiser."

It all made sense, and a good meal sounded great after a week of Twinkies and potato chips, so off we went to see the sights of Roma.

The town was just like a dozen others we had hurried through in south Texas - boring and uninviting. The people seemed to be mostly ranch hands, more than half of them Chicano. The downtown consisted of a general store/post office, a gas station, a used car dealership, a feed and tack store, and one Mexican restaurant. We pulled up and parked out front. We did the best we could to straighten ourselves up, then went in.

It was a clean place, with red checked tablecloths and lighted beer signs on the walls. Each table had dishes of salsa and pickled carrots and jalapenos. There were two other tables occupied, one by four older white guys and one by a Chicano family. They sat at opposite ends of the restaurant. Both conversations stopped when we came in. We took a table midway between them.

The waitress, a short middle-aged Chicana, brought us our menus and tried politely not to stare at us. We ordered chips and a pitcher of Dos Equis to start. At first we spoke in whispers, feeling very out of place. The other diners stared at us but no one said anything or looked particularly hostile, and after a while we loosened up.

By the second pitcher of beer we were feeling fine. There was good Mariachi music on the jukebox, the food was great, and the waitress even laughed with us once or twice.

"See?" said Sean. "There was nothing to worry about. These are good country people; salt of the earth. Living in cities has just made us paranoid."

"Yeah," Mike agreed. "They probably never heard of hippies. They don't know about making a sociopolitical statement with your personal style. You couldn't explain it to them in a million years. They probably just think we're from Mars or something."

Mike and Sean got into a thing with the jalapenos. We'd each tried a bite, so we knew they were hot. I was still sweating from the one I'd eaten. Sean said they must be about the hottest in the world.

"Nah, these are nothing," said Mike. "Back in Nam they have these tiny little red ones that are ten times hotter than these."

"Bullshit," said Sean. "No one could eat 'em."

"Hell, yes. I ate plenty of them. I ate 'em like peanuts."

"Come on. If they were ten times hotter than these, it'd be like eating ten of these all at once. That'd kill anybody."

"No, it wouldn't. You don't know what you're talking about."

"Of course it would. No one could eat ten jalapenos."

"I could."

"Shit. I'd like to see you try."

"Ten bucks?"

Sean looked at him. That was probably more than half of his life's savings right now. On the other hand, tomorrow he would be rich. He was also getting tired of Mike's stuff about how tough everything in Nam had been. Also he was getting drunk.

"Right." He dug a ten out of his pocket and smoothed it out on the table.

I secretly agreed it couldn't be done, but Mike didn't bat an eye. He matched the bet and pulled the jalapenos in front of him.

"Mike," said Elissa. "Don't be silly. They'll burn a hole right through you."

"Shut up," said Chris. "I want to see this."

"Okay, ye of little faith, watch this," said Mike. He picked out a pepper and popped it in his mouth, chewing vigorously. Beads of sweat popped out on his forehead, but he showed no sign of discomfort. He swallowed quickly and reached for another.

"One," he said.

He went on gamely enough through five, but his face was fiery red and sweat was running down into his eyes. He seemed to have lost his voice, but Sean took up the count.

"Six. Four more."

By this time the other patrons had noticed what was going on. Everyone stopped eating to watch as Mike ate seven, then eight. I heard the Mexican father mutter "Ay, caramba."

Mike looked terrible. His whole face was swollen. He could barely open his eyes. Tears and sweat dripped from his chin. We stared in fascination as he downed number nine.

"Nine. One to go," Sean tolled.

"Mike, for God's sake," I said, "it's not worth it." He picked out the smallest remaining pepper and peered at it half-blind, then dropped it on his tongue. He gave a gulp and swallowed it whole.

"Jesus Christ," said Sean. "The silly shit really did it."

Mike grinned triumphantly for a split second, then he sobered and looked startled. He jumped up, knocking over his chair, and bolted out the door. We rushed after him while the bunch of white guys broke up laughing behind us.

We found Mike bent over the curb, throwing up a violently green mess into the gutter. After he finally recovered, we led him back in and he drank the rest of the third pitcher of beer. Sean was heartless enough to bring up the point that he hadn't technically consumed the ten jalapenos, but the rest of us berated him and he paid up.

We quickly finished up our dinner, paid, and left. It occurred to us that perhaps we could have kept a lower profile by not throwing up on their town, but there seemed to be no harm done other than to Mike's digestive tract.

Sean drove back west, past the power line. He went quite a way, probably five miles, before he found an ungated dirt road. About a mile in, the rutted track ended at a tumble down cattle chute. He backed the car in against the rotted wood fence. It was a bitter cold night, with a clear dark sky. Sean and Chris crawled in back with Mike, Elissa, and me. We filled the pipe extra full and added some hash and a chunk of opium. In honor of the occasion, I even sprinkled in most of the last of my DMT, dimethyl tryptamine, a short-lived but quite intense smokable psychedelic. We proceeded to get royally loaded, laughing and telling stories late into the night. Sometime in the wee hours we passed out, sprawled across one another as usual.

Chapter Six
Vigilantes

I woke with Elissa shaking me.

"Brian, wake up! There's a car coming!"

I sat up groggily. "What? Where? I don't see anything."

"It's behind that rise now. I couldn't sleep and then car lights came in the windows. I sat up in time to see it go down behind that hill. It's coming up this road, I know it." She sounded scared, and I couldn't blame her. Why would somebody be coming back on this old dirt road in the middle of the night? We woke up the others. Soon we were all lined up peering out the windows, our bare butts in a row. Sure enough, a moment later a car crested the hill and started bumping down toward us.

"Shit. How could anybody know we're here?"

"I don't know. Is the car locked?"

"The back door doesn't lock," said Chris.

"What?" squeaked Elissa. "We can't keep them out?"

"Not if they want in," said Sean.

We watched terrified as the car approached. My only hope was that they were ranch hands going to work or something. Not likely. The lights came right at us, blinding us, then stopped, blocking us against the corral behind us. We couldn't get out even if we could get to the cab. We heard four car doors slam.

Ouch, four of them, at least. Not that a bunch of stoned out pacifist hippies were likely to fight off even one redneck bent on murder. Silhouettes moved across in front of the lights. There were long diagonal lines among the moving shadows.

"Oh, shit," said Chris. "They've got guns." I suddenly felt even colder.

We heard footsteps crunching in the gravel on both sides of the car. We all held our breaths. Would they just start shooting?

Suddenly the back door was yanked open and two brilliant flashlights dazzled us. The girls screamed. The warm humid air of the car poured out and the icy night air rushed in. We pulled the bedding up to our necks. My heart was pounding like a jackhammer. I desperately tried to think what I could say or do to get out of this one.

"Out of the car, all of you!" growled a harsh voice.

What could we do? First Mike, then Sean and I scrambled out and stood naked and shivering in the lights. We couldn't see anything of our attackers, not even how many there were.

"Listen," I began, "we have women here. Let them stay in the..."

"Shut up! Everybody out!"

Finally Elissa and Chris climbed out, trying to cover themselves. Someone whistled in the dark. Elissa was whimpering. All of us were shivering with cold and pure terror. Nothing makes you feel more helpless and vulnerable than being naked. We couldn't even run away into the desert like this. One of the lights dropped for a moment and I caught a glimpse of the end of a two-by-four waving menacingly. My heart sank even lower. What would it feel like to be beaten to death with that thing?

"What are you doing here?"

"We're just camping," said Sean. "We needed a place to sleep. We'll be leaving at dawn." We all prayed that was still true.

"Where are you from?"

"Different places. We're just traveling together."

"Where are you traveling to?"

"Albuquerque, some of us. Some to LA."

"But you came into town from the west." How the hell did they know that?

These weren't just ranch hands who had stumbled on us. They'd known we were here and had come looking for us.

"Oh. Oh, yeah. We decided we couldn't make it to Laredo, so we turned back to camp."

"But first you stopped to eat at Ramona's."

"Yeah, we were hungry. Did we do something wrong?"

"Damn right you did something wrong. You came into Texas. We don't like your kind around here. You're not welcome here."

"We'd be happy to move along."

"Shut up! Do you own this car?"

"Yeah."

"This your wife?" The muzzle of an over-and-under thrust into the light, pointing between Elissa's breasts. She was crying.

"No. That's my lady over there. Chris."

"She's with me," I said, and discovered my voice was breaking with fright.

One of the lights came up into my face. I squinted into the glare.

"Shit," said the voice. "With hair like that ah thought ya wuz a girl, but ah can see ya ain't." Someone else laughed in the dark. "I can't figure how faggoty scumbags like you guys have such good-looking women." I decided not to use any of several snappy retorts that came to mind. I figured we were only a few minutes or one smart-ass comment from a multiple rape and murder. Our lives depended on answering these questions satisfactorily. Who were these guys, and what did they want? I couldn't guess and didn't want to ask. The only part I was happy about was that the beating hadn't started yet.

"Listen to me, all of you," said their leader. "I don't know what you're doing here, but we don't like you and we don't want you around here. If we ever see you around here again, we'll kill you. Got that?"

I was so relieved to hear that they might see us again that I didn't even mind the death threat. It meant that they planned to let us go. But I was still afraid, especially for the women. They could still rape the girls just to teach us a lesson, and there wasn't a damn thing we could do to prevent it.

"So here's what's going to happen," the voice continued. We were all ears, believe me. "You're going to get in that car and drive west, out of Roma, out of Starr County, out of Texas. You won't stop, you won't slow down, you won't look back. We'll be watching to see that you do. You've got one minute before we stop feeling so friendly. Now git!"

We didn't have to be told twice. Sean and Chris grabbed some blankets out of the back and jumped in the cab. The rest of us piled in the back. As our assailants went back to their car, I could see there were four of them. They all carried some kind of weapon. They started their car and started turning around, giving us room to get out.

It took Sean three tries to get the car started while the rest of us shouted at him, then it finally roared to life. He popped the clutch and we rolled against the back door as he shot down that rutted dirt track as fast as that old ambulance could go. He hit the highway and fishtailed as he headed west with the accelerator floored. The other car followed us a few hundred yards behind.

Elissa was still crying. We were all chilled to the bone and struggled into our clothes as we bounced around in the back. We found Sean and Chris's clothes and passed them through the window with some extra blankets. We were all very aware of the lights following us.

The car followed us another ten minutes, then pulled over to the side and turned off its lights. Elissa was just shouting to Chris that they were gone, when another car turned on its lights and pulled out behind us. They must have been waiting for us, stationed there to make sure we kept going. Somehow that scared me as much as anything else that had happened. These guys weren't just good old boys out to scare some hippies; they were organized. How many of them were there, for Christ's sake? It seemed as if the whole county was out to get us.

Sean drove on into the night. After another ten minutes or so the second car turned off its lights and stopped. We waited for another, but we seemed finally to be alone on the highway. Sean drove another fifteen minutes, then pulled over and he and Chris joined us in back so they could get dressed. His teeth were chattering.

"Damn, man," said Mike. "That's the last time I do DMT. That shit's a bad trip."

"Can you believe those guys? What's their trip, anyway?"

"I was so scared I almost peed myself."

"Me too. I was afraid I'd have a pissicle down my leg."

"Damn, that was scary. Let's get going again."

"Oh, they've given up. We're okay here."

"You know what really bums me out?" said Mike. "We finally found the peyote fields, we know right where it is, and we just can't go pick it."

"Yeah," said Sean. "All that money just a few miles away and all we had to do was pick it up off the ground."

"All those buttons," I agreed sadly.

"Fuck the peyote," said Elissa. "Let's get out of here. I don't want to see those guys again."

"I knew we shouldn't have gone to that damn restaurant," said Chris.

"We should have just camped out there, hiked in and picked it during the day, and beat it by dark."

"Yeah, no one could see us out in the fields. We'd be all right once we were in there."

"But we couldn't leave the car parked by the road. The boys would be waiting for us with nooses."

"Yeah, it's the car that's so conspicuous."

"Let's talk about it later," said Elissa again. "Let's go."

"You know the one place in the world those guys would not expect us to be tomorrow?" asked Mike. "Roma."

"They'd be right," said Chris.

"But look. If we went back right now…"

"Went back?" Elissa screeched.

"Listen to me. If we went back now while it's still dark no one would ever know. Those guys have no clue what we were after, I'm sure of it. They'd never guess we'd go back, especially so soon. We could go to the road by the fields and drop three or four people off with lots of bags and containers."

"I can't believe you're even suggesting..." began Elissa.

"Then we could beat it the hell out with the car - get far, far away."

"Yeah," said Chris, getting into it now. "The guys in the fields should be safe enough. That's just empty range land out there, and you can't see it from the road or the town."

"And the car could come back and pick them up right after dark," Mike continued. "We could be out of beloved Starr County by midnight with a carload of peyote and be flying high to LA all the way."

"And into druggie history with the boldest score ever." I was getting excited about it too now.

"That's not bold, that's stupid," complained Elissa. "You guys are crazy to even be talking about it. Those guys would kill us. They said so."

"Only if they catch us, and they won't even be looking for us. By now they're home in bed, screwing their fat old ladies and fantasizing about you girls. We won't even get within sight of the town. It'll be a quick raid, a surgical strike, a quick in and out."

"I'm worried about the quick in and out we'll get if those guys catch us."

"Let's vote on it," I said. "Who's for going back?" Everyone voted aye except Elissa.

"Okay, that's settled," said Mike. "Now, who's going to do the picking?"

"I need to drive the car," said Sean, though I couldn't see why he always insisted on doing all the driving. Nevertheless, it was his car and I was only a passenger.

"I'm having nothing to do with it," said Elissa. "I'm not getting out of the car until we're in California. I'll pee out the window from now on."

"Okay," I said. "So Chris, Mike and I hit the desert before dawn and pick like mad all day."

"Uh, no, I don't think I want to go out there," said Chris.

"Damn," said Mike. "We could pick lots more with three of us."

"She said she doesn't want to go, okay?" said Sean. Mike shrugged.

"Right, are we all agreed?" I asked.

"I agree you're all crazy," said Elissa, "but like I said, I'm not getting out of this car."

"Okay," said Mike. "So it's just Brian and me. Anybody got the time?"

Sean stuck his head through the window to see the dashboard clock. "It's four-thirty."

"The sun comes up about six-thirty in the winter, right? We want to get there while it's still completely dark so the car can be well away before first light. Say, five forty-five. It's about forty-five minutes back to the fields. That means we should start back at five, about half an hour from now."

That gave me pause. Now it wasn't something we were talking about doing tomorrow, it was right now. I tried to decide whether this was completely stupid or just terribly risky. Part of me wanted to do it just because it was wild and crazy. Part of me was terrified. But it was humiliating to be threatened and chased away by those assholes. We couldn't fight them, but this would salvage the purpose of our trip and prove, at least to me, that we weren't completely helpless against these Texas vigilantes. It seemed that with plenty of chutzpah and any luck at all it should work.

Chapter Seven
The Heist

We were too wired to sleep, but we ate some sandwiches and crackers. Then we emptied everybody's duffel bag out, adding to the tangle of clothes and stuff that half filled the car. We found four or five sleeping bags that didn't have any large tears in them. Altogether we had ten bags, plus we could tie up our coats and make two more if necessary. It would be a load to carry, but Mike and I figured we could make several trips back to the road with the full bags. We would have about twelve hours in the fields, which should give us plenty of time.

At five o'clock Sean and Chris got back in the cab and we headed back toward Roma. We were peering out the windows, watching for cars parked along the road, but there were none.

Mike's calculations had been slightly off. We had gone further than any of us had guessed in our high-speed flight. The sky was noticeably pink in the east before we came within sight of the high-tension lines. The car slid to a stop beside the ramshackle gate. Elissa kissed me, and Mike and I tumbled out. The girls tossed all the bags out after us.

"We'll be back as soon as it gets completely dark!" shouted Sean through the window. Then the car kicked up gravel and dust as it made a fast U-turn and disappeared to the west. We threw all the bags over the gate, jumped after them, and dragged everything down under some bushes out of sight of the road to wait for light.

Nothing happened. We waited maybe fifteen minutes until there was enough light to be able to walk. We gathered up armloads of bags and trudged off into the desert.

It was rough country, thickly grown with chaparral, sagebrush, prickly pear, and mesquite, most of it about shoulder high. There was enough sandy space between the bushes to walk easily, but the bags were constantly getting caught on the thorns and we'd have to rip them free. We went maybe a mile before we got to the power lines, then threw everything down to take a break. Mike climbed part way up the tower.

"That's Roma over that next ridge," he said. "So this is the second ridge from town. If the peyote man was right, the fields should be just over that ridge to the west."

"Let's do it," I said. "I want to see the stuff. If we're wrong about this, we've risked our asses for nothing."

We picked up all the bags again and struggled on down the hill, following the power lines. We had to cross a steep arroyo at the bottom, then back up the other side. When we got to the top of the next ridge we were probably two miles from the road. The next valley looked exactly like the last.

"Is this it?" I asked. "Doesn't look any different."

"What did you expect, the leaning tower of peyote? They're small, man. Let's go. And keep your eyes open."

We started slowly down the hill, our eyes scanning the ground. The sun was just about to break the horizon, so the light was adequate.

There are a lot of small, low growing cacti, we discovered. One in particular looks very similar to peyote, but doesn't have the little white dots of thorns. Since neither of us had ever seen live peyote on the hoof, we weren't exactly sure what it would look like. Mike saw the first one.

"Hey! Hey, Brian, here's one!"

I hurried over. There under a big prickly pear was a peyote button, looking just like the ones we'd eaten, but fresher and greener and rounder. It was three inches across and stuck up maybe an inch above the ground. I got out my penknife and sliced it off at the ground. The cut root was yellow-green and oozed wet. We examined the button, passing it back and forth.

"That's peyote, all right. We're here, man. We are here!"

We grinned at each other. The sun came up behind us.

"Let's get picking."

We continued down the hillside, picking as we went. They got thicker and thicker, until the ground was literally covered with them. We could hardly put our feet down without stepping on one. Long before I reached the bottom of the slope I had filled the first bag. I tied it closed and left it, figuring we'd pick them up on our way back. The bag was heavy, and I realized we had a job ahead of us lugging all those bags back to the road. We'd have a hard time carrying more than one at a time.

I became more selective. The biggest ones grew way in under the prickly pears; a nasty spot because the ground there was covered with old dried prickly pear thorns. It was slow, awkward work, reaching in under the pear trees to dig out the big four- and five-inch buttons. But they filled the bags faster than the little ones.

Mike and I had each filled two more bags by the time we reached the next arroyo. At this rate we'd be loaded by noon and should have plenty of time to drag them all back to the road before dark. This damn caper was going to work.

"You know?" said Mike, invisible a few bushes away. "I just remembered. The Indians say you're supposed to eat the first buttons you find right away to appease the gods of peyote."

"Oh, great," I called back. "Now you tell me. What if you don't?"

"I don't know. The gods bring you bad luck, I guess."

"Or bad trips. Maybe we should eat one now just to be sure."

"Sounds okay to me." He walked over and we sat down together on the sand. We each took out the biggest buttons we'd found recently. They were giants; as big as my hand and twice as thick.

"We thank the gods for sending us this powerful magic," said Mike, holding up the buttons like offerings. "We eat them with respect and apologize for killing your sacred cactus."

We cut off the fuzz and ate them like apples. They weren't as slimy and disgusting fresh, but the taste was if anything even stronger than we'd remembered - and we'd remembered it a lot. But in the solemn spirit of the ceremony we chewed them up thoroughly. Then we figured the gods wouldn't mind a little chaser to kill the taste and had melted Reese cups and long drinks of water. Then we went back to picking, working up the next slope.

We were nearly to the top of the ridge and were just filling our next bags when I heard an engine. Mike was further up the slope and a hundred yards to my right. I saw him straighten up and look around. The sound came again, louder. Suddenly a light green Jeep topped the first ridge. We both hit the dirt and peered through the brush. The Jeep disappeared into the intervening valley, heading our way.

"Shit," I yelled. "Who's that?"

"I don't know, but they'll be over that hill in a couple of minutes and we better be out of sight." Mike threw his half-full sleeping bag over his shoulder and bounded off through the brush to our left, circling around to get behind the hill. I did the same on a lower track. I could hear the Jeep's engine again, obviously working hard climbing the hill. We plowed wildly ahead, tearing our clothes and skin on the sharp thorns on every bush, our feet sliding on the steep gravelly slope, the heavy bags bouncing on our backs. The engine sound came louder, and I knew it was coming over the hill behind us.

Then we were around the hill, out of sight. We continued running, angling downward now, trying to get to the arroyo at the bottom, which offered at least a hope of finding shelter in this open country. The sound of the Jeep got louder again. Any second it was going to come out on top of our hill and we'd be dead men. I dropped the bag and ran as hard as I could, my breath rasping in my lungs. Out of the corner of my eye I could see Mike doing the same thing, though he was still a hundred yards or so above me and to my right. Then beyond him I saw a glint of light at the top of the hill. We both threw ourselves down into the dirt.

I scrambled in under a big mesquite, ignoring the thorns. The engine idled, then stopped. I was still close enough to hear the ping of metal as the engine cooled.

Looking up through the brush, I could see a man get out of the Jeep. He had on a green uniform and a wide flat-brimmed hat like a ranger. I was relieved - at least it wasn't the vigilantes we'd encountered during the night.

The man looked down the hillside in our direction, then reached into the Jeep and brought out a pair of binoculars. For several long minutes he scanned the hill, looking right towards us. I was pretty sure he hadn't seen us when he crested the hill, and there was still a good chance he wouldn't find us. There were thousands of bushes on that hill, and only two of them sheltered terrified hippies.

Then he put down the glasses and started walking right toward us. I couldn't believe it. I only caught a few glimpses of him after that, but each time he was closer and still walking right at me. I slithered deeper under the mesquite. Then I heard a voice, close enough for me to clearly hear what was said.

"What you doing down there, boy?"

My heart sank. He'd found Mike! But I still harbored a faint hope that he didn't know there were two of us. I hoped I could count on Mike to be cool.

"I... I...," I heard Mike stammer. "Um, picking fruit?"

I stuffed my fist in my mouth to keep from laughing or crying, I wasn't sure which.

"Picking them pye-oaties, looks to me."

Damn. This country cop was smarter than I had counted on. I had been making up excuses for trespassing.

"Where's your buddy?"

"Nobody here but me, officer, sir," said Mike. Thanks, brother.

"Waal, let's just mosey down here a little farther, what say? Come on." I lay trembling as I heard them coming through the brush, their footsteps getting louder and louder. Finally I saw black boots come around a big prickly pear and walk right up to the mesquite where I lay. The guy must have built-in radar for hippies.

"Waal, looky here. Another one. Come on out of there, you rascal." I squirmed out from under the bush and stood up. The dude was tall and lean and weathered, with none of the potbelly and tobacco chewing I associated with Southern cops. Then I saw his arm patch - Immigration and Naturalization! This wasn't some country cop. This was La Migra!

He led us back to the Jeep, stopping to pick up the bags we'd dropped. I noticed one of our other bags in the back of the Jeep. They no longer contained a fortune in great dope, I realized - they held evidence. Hell, I'd had friends get fifteen years in the state pen for one marijuana seed. What did you get for hundreds of peyote buttons? I could already hear the judge: Did you obtain any evidence of their guilt? Yes sir, yes sir, three bags full. No doubt about it. We were goners.

He sat us down on the ground, one beside each front wheel, then handcuffed us, running the cuffs through the holes in the wheels. He got himself a drink of water from a cooler in the back, then got on his radio.

"Unit nine to base."

I heard the radio crackle, but couldn't make out the other side of the conversation.

"I got two hippies out here. Been picking them peyotes. Yuh. Yuh. Okay. Well, I'll just stand by out here till you get back to me. Okay. Ten-four."

He came around then and gave each of us a swallow of water. It was after noon now, and hot in the sun. We sat dejectedly, too depressed to talk.

"Hey, officer," I heard Mike call from the other side of the Jeep.

"Yeah?"

"How did you know we were out there?"

"Plane spotted you an hour ago. Damn river's just over that hill there. We always patrol this stretch with the plane. He said he saw two people, I come out to pick up the wetbacks and find you two. Just lucky, I guess."

Some luck, I thought. Maybe this was because we hadn't eaten the first buttons we found. Shit, that's right. We should be coming on to a powerful trip any minute. My stomach was already feeling queasy. Oh, great. Just when I thought it couldn't get any worse. The radio crackled again. He thumbed the mike.

"Unit nine. Hi, chief. Two of them. Yuh. Yuh. The same ones we talked to last night. Yuh, the hairy one and the bald one. No sign of the others or the car."

My despair reached new depths. I'd been relieved to see that it was a cop, not a vigilante. Worse yet, it was both. Well, they'd already told us what would happen if they caught us again. I had a sudden image of him just taking off in the Jeep, flailing us to death until there was nothing left but bloody handcuffs.

"Yuh, so what do we do with 'em? Wanna give Ramon a call? Okay, I'll bring 'em in for now. Out."

"Okay, into the car," he told us, freeing us from the wheels. We clambered into the back of the Jeep, sitting on top of our bags of buttons. He handcuffed us to the grab rail behind the seat and took off. It was all we could do to keep from being thrown out of the car. It seemed to take forever to get back to the road, but finally the jouncing stopped and he pulled out onto the road, heading east, through Roma, and beyond.

"Where are we going?" I shouted above the wind.

"Border Patrol at Rio Grande City," he called over his shoulder. I decided that was good news. If they were going to kill us, it would probably have been back there in the desert. Now all we had to worry about was spending the rest of our lives in jail.

Chapter Eight
Rio Grande City Jail

We rolled along the south Texas highway, the sun bright above us, the wind whipping my hair. It was rather pleasant, probably enhanced by the fact that the peyote was really coming on strong now. It felt almost like an outing, a ride in a convertible. But I was on my way to jail. This could be my last ride in the open air for many years, perhaps forever.

The drug underground had legends about many of the famous prisons that had swallowed up so many of our comrades. I knew some bad stories about Joliet in Illinois, but everybody seemed to agree that the worst pen in the country was Huntsville, Texas, where sadistic guards with shotguns and cattle prods drive the prisoners as they pick cotton in the noonday sun until they drop. Mose Allison wrote a song about the eleven-foot cotton sacks you drag with you. Now I was going to find out what that was like.

We arrived in Rio Grande City. The officer parked there and went in, leaving us alone in the Jeep. A crowd of Chicano kids gathered around us.

"Hey, heepies. What you do?"

"Nothing," said Mike. "The capitalist overlords are trying to crush the resistance movement, just as they oppress minority peoples everywhere. But they can never win. If they kill us, a hundred more will rise up in our place. We are everywhere, living in their cities, infiltrating their armed forces, sleeping with their daughters. Death to the pigs! You are our brothers in arms, noble sons of Moctezuma. Set us free and we will lead you to freedom."

All of us stared at Mike in amazement. I looked at the kids and they looked at me.

"Sheet. These guys is loco," said one, and they wandered off.

Jim came out of the office and climbed back into the Jeep. He turned and looked at us.

"There's no Federal law against picking peyote, so we're turning you over to the Starr County sheriff." We drove off again.

I didn't know if that was good or bad. As alienated as I was from the American government, its laws, foreign policy, and wars, I was still young and American enough to think that it abided by its own laws. I thought I'd at least get a trial. But I had bad images of southern sheriffs, usually guffawing along with the other good old boys as somebody was lynched.

We turned off on a side street and parked behind an old courthouse. We were led up the back stairs to a barred door.

A Chicano man in a sheriff's uniform came to the door. He was short and round and had a pleasant, friendly face.

"Hi, Jim. These the two Bob called me about?"

"Yuh. Got three bags of cactus out in the car, too."

"Damn. What am I going to do with that? It's Saturday. It'll start to smell before I can get 'em to court."

"Dunno, Luis. But it's evidence. You gotta keep it."

"You can put it in our cell," said Mike. "We don't mind."

I thought that crack might result in a gun butt to the head, but to my surprise they both laughed.

"Don't suppose you'd smell any the worse for it," said Jim. The sheriff led us in and put us in a holding tank while he and Jim did the transfer paperwork. Jim took off our handcuffs, which was a real relief. We looked around at our new home.

It was clean and well lighted and there was a regular toilet, not one of those stand-up commodes you get in some jails. It was a long rectangular cage built against two brick walls. Through the bars we could look through an open door into what appeared to be the sheriff's living room. His kids were watching TV. I thought it strange that he lived in the courthouse next to the jail, but I supposed it must be convenient. After a while Jim left and Luis went back into his house. He left the door open, maybe so we could watch TV, we weren't sure.

Mike and I talked about our situation and admitted we were dead meat. There wasn't a hint of a defense in sight. On the other hand, we weren't being mistreated and we were in the most comfortable digs we'd been in for a long while. It felt nice to relax in bed and chat with Mike. Except for an occasional paranoid fantasy, he'd been pretty quiet on the trip down and I didn't have a feel for him at all, but with nothing else to do we talked a lot.

He'd been just an ordinary kid, growing up in LA, messing around with pot and rock'n'roll, listening to Dylan and the Beatles and the Stones, gradually getting his head straightened around from the bending they put on it in school. Then something terrible happened: he graduated from high school. Within two weeks he was on his way to Indochina, as they called it then.

He'd gotten off the plane in Da Nang and was sitting around on a pile of luggage with a bunch of the other recruits, looking around at the strange new country and talking about how hot it was. Then a mortar shell landed and blew the guy he was talking to into hamburger and messed up a bunch more. Those guys were just put back on the same plane and shipped home, one in a very nearly empty body bag. After that, he said, it got worse. He didn't tell me too many more details, but the way he said it made me glad he didn't want to talk about it any more.

He'd survived a year, then gone off the deep end and been shipped home on a Section Eight. Again, he didn't give me the details, but he did say other guys were shooting off their toes so they could go home, so I guess it isn't easy to get a Section Eight. He got off the plane in Seattle and couldn't imagine just going home and hanging with the guys, so he hit the road. Now, at nineteen, he was flat broke and was heading for home. Or he had been before this little contretemps with the law.

Later a wonderful smell wafted from the sheriff's house - home-cooked Mexican food. Our mouths watered. We hadn't eaten since the meal at Ramona's the night before. We expected somebody to pour a bucket of swill into the cell or something, but soon a nice-looking Chicana lady came out with two huge steaming plates of enchiladas and beans. I'm sure it was the same thing her family was eating.

"Gracias, Senora, gracias," called Mike as she was leaving. "Delicioso!" She turned and smiled.

"Dos cervezas, por favor," I tried, and she laughed with us before returning to her family.

"Damn, man," I mumbled with my mouth full of beans, "is this a great jail or what?"

"Best time I ever did," agreed Mike. We ate well and slept soundly in soft clean beds for a change.

The sheriff brought us our breakfast (machaca and fried eggs) in the morning.

"Well, boys," he said. "Today's Sunday and there's no court today. The judge will see you first thing Monday morning. In the meantime I'll let you out one at a time to take showers and get cleaned up. My wife will wash your clothes if you want."

That was the first time I realized that it was at least a week since my last bath and I'd been living, sleeping, and running around in the desert all that time in the same clothes. I bet all of us in that ambulance must have been pretty rank. Fortunately, we all smelled just as bad, so nobody minded.

As neither of us had other clothes, the sheriff loaned us a couple of his son's jeans and shirts. By the afternoon we were bathed and had clean clothes and I had put my hair in a conservative waist-length braid. We had two more great meals and spent a while chatting with the sheriff's young boy who came into the jail to stare at us. We were feeling almost happy about being busted.

The next morning the sheriff took us down the hall to the courtroom. Now we were nervous again. Huntsville was still a possibility. There were five or six other people in the courtroom, but I didn't know if they were awaiting trial or had just come to watch a hanging. The judge came in, a rather fierce-looking older dude with a white moustache. The sheriff led us up before him.

"Monday, February 16th, 1968," he announced. "State of Texas versus Crawford and Simpson, your honor. Possession of a controlled substance."

The judge looked us up and down curiously. I felt quite sure he'd never seen a hippie outside of Time magazine.

"What substance?" he asked.

"Peyote, your honor," said the sheriff.

"What the hell's that?"

"It's a cactus, your honor."

"A cactus? What do they use it for?"

"It's a narcotic, your honor."

"A narcotic cactus? Never heard of it." He stared at us. "Where you boys from?"

"I'm from Ohio, your honor," I said. "I'm a college student, majoring in geology. I'm on vacation, between terms." He cocked an eyebrow at that. I guess I didn't look like a college boy to him. I was certainly no Aggie.

"I'm from Los Angeles, sir," said Mike. "I'm a GI, a combat veteran just returned from serving my country in Vietnam." I thought that was a nice touch. Mike was handling himself well. I'd been afraid he'd start off about capitalist oppression.

"And if I may be allowed to make one statement?" he continued. My heart sank. Huntsville, here we come.

"Peyote, or *Lophophora williamsii*, is not a narcotic. It is an hallucinogen, sacred to the Native American peoples, and is…"

"Hold it right there, boy. Sheriff, have you looked up the statutes on this stuff?"

"All I know is it's a controlled substance under article 7449."

"Okay. That's all I need to know. Where's your evidence?"

"The INS picked them up down by the river. They had bags of the stuff. It's out back. I can bring it in, but it's gone off. You wouldn't like it in here."

"No, that's okay. Looks like we got you boys dead to rights. Do you deny you were picking this… what is it?"

"*Lophophora williamsii*" began Mike.

"Whatever. Do you deny it?"

"No, your honor," we both said. What was the point of denying it?

"Okay, that's it. I find you guilty of possession of this here controlled substance. I fine you both twenty-five dollars. Pay the clerk and get out of town."

I couldn't believe it. Twenty-five bucks? I thought it would be twenty-five years. The judge turned over a paper on his desk and started reading the next case.

"Uh, your honor, sir?" Mike said.

The judge scowled over his glasses at him.

"I don't have twenty-five dollars."

I shook my head. "Me either."

"Well, the jail rate is five dollars a day. If you can't pay the fine, you'll have to do five days in jail. Do you still claim you don't have the money?"

"Yes, sir," we both nodded. "We'll take the time, your honor," I said.

"Dammit, judge," said the sheriff. "Do I have to feed these locos for five more days?"

"That's the law, Luis. They're not above the law, and neither are we." He turned back to us. "I sentence you each to five days in Starr County Jail. That's until five PM on Friday. Take 'em away, Luis."

The sheriff glumly led us back to our cell. When he was gone, I turned and grinned at Mike.

"Boy, he really threw the book at us, didn't he?"

"Damn," yelled Mike. "This is great! Five days of this great Mexican food."

We flopped on our beds and relaxed, free of fear for the first time since coming into Texas. Our main concern now was what had happened to the others. Also, of course, all our stuff was in the car. We decided we'd seen the last of it all.

But late that afternoon the sheriff stuck his head in to tell us we had a visitor. Puzzled, we went to the bars. Elissa came out of the sheriff's apartment, looking scared but beautiful.

"Baby!" I yelled, "What are you doing here?"

"The police told us you were here," she said.

"But how did you ask them? Where have you been?"

"After we dropped you guys off we drove west a few miles, then Sean decided we'd go down to the river and go fishing. There's a big lake there, Falcon Reservoir. At least it would give us an excuse for being there if anybody saw us. In late afternoon a Border Patrol truck showed up. They came over and said our friends were in Rio Grande City jail and we could visit you the next day if we wanted to. They were really nice."

"How did they know you were there? We didn't even know."

"I don't know. We couldn't figure it out either. They didn't hassle or us search us or even question us. They did suggest we not stay in south Texas any longer. It was spooky, like they knew everything we had done since we came."

"I know," I agreed. "They've got an organization here. It's weird."

"It's the CIA," said Mike. "They run this big cocaine smuggling operation from South America and use the money to prop up puppet dictatorships in Central America. They need this border in their control. Nothing happens within a hundred miles of the border that they don't know about. They've got La Migra and the Border Patrol in their pay, too."

We looked at him blankly. Where did Mike get all that stuff? I thought it unlikely then, figuring it was another of his crackpot conspiracy theories, though later events have shown that he was probably right.

"So what are you going to do?" I asked Elissa.

"Sean and Chris want to leave right away. They've heard there's a hippie scene in Fort Worth and they want to go check it out. I want to stay with you."

"You can't stay here alone for five days until we get out. You should stay with them."

"But how will we get together again? And what about your stuff?"

"You keep it. When we get out we'll go to Fort Worth, too. I'll try to find you. If there is a scene there it can't be too big. Put the word out about where you're staying and I'll find you. If we can't hook up, sell my stuff for what you can get and buy a bus ticket to California. The guitar should be worth that in a pawn shop."

"But how will you get to Fort Worth? We've only got twenty dollars left."

"Let's split it. Mike and I can hitch there when we get out."

Elissa wasn't happy about going off by herself. She'd never really liked Sean and Chris and thought she couldn't trust them. But she sure couldn't stay in Rio Grande City, so she agreed to the plan.

"I'll go get the money," she said. "Anything else you want out of your stuff?"

"Yeah," I said. "My heavy coat." Then a wild thought struck me. "Oh, yeah. And my sample case."

"What? Your dope samples? In here? Are you crazy?"

"No, I think it'll be okay. The sheriff is really nice and doesn't hassle us at all. He only comes in once a day to make sure we're still here. Besides, I don't want you holding while you're traveling with Sean and Chris. They might try to rip you off."

"You really think it's safe?" she asked, not at all convinced.

"Sure," said Mike. "It'll be cool. They'd never suspect it. They already searched us when we came in. They're not going to search us on the way out."

"Well, okay, if you're sure." She went back out to the car where Sean and Chris were waiting impatiently. They were spooked about being at the jail and just wanted to get out of town. In a few minutes Elissa was back with my pea coat over her arm.

"Your money's in the pocket," she said as she pushed it through the bars.

"Thanks, babe," I said. "You're a doll."

She looked at me sadly. Her lip was trembling.

"I can't stand to leave you here like this," she said, her voice breaking.

"It's the only way, babe. You'll be all right. I'll see you in a week in Fort Worth. Find a nice safe crash house, put out the word, and wait for me." I gave her a long kiss and a squeeze through the bars and she hugged me back hard. Then she went out, turning at the door to say goodbye to Mike and throw me a kiss. The sheriff never reappeared. God, I love lax security.

I checked the pockets of my coat. There was my ten-dollar bill, tucked in with four or five plastic boxes of various drugs. We were set.

The first thing both of us did was to write home for cash. I had a joint checking account with my mother that still had a couple hundred in it, so I asked her to close it out and wire me the money. I'm sure she was really pleased to see a jail as my return address. Mike wrote to his mom in LA, asking her to send what she could.

When the sheriff stopped in at dinnertime we asked him for some smoke. He came back a few minutes later with a bag of Bull Durham, some papers, and a box of matches. He was a fine man. After another wonderful meal we smoked a few joints, carefully exhaling out the window.

Chapter Nine
The Locals

After dinner the sheriff came back to say we had another visitor. We looked at each other in surprise. Who in the world could it be?

A kid about sixteen came in and sat on the bench just outside the bars. He was tall and skinny and had bad acne, but he had an intelligent look in his eye. He smiled shyly at us.

"Hi. I'm Billy."

"Pleased to meet you, Billy," Mike said. "I'm Mike and this is Brian."

Billy reached through the bars to shake hands. Mike gave him the hippie handshake, which only confused him. I gave him five.

"I guess you're wondering why I'm here," Billy said, and we nodded.

"I'm a freshman out at the local JC," he began. "My girlfriend Alicia was in court for speeding yesterday and she saw you there. She'd never seen anybody like you guys around here."

"Nobody like us has ever been here before," said Mike.

"Well, she told me about you. She knew I was interested in hippies and stuff. Are you guys really hippies?" He asked it with such hope in his face. Far be it from me to disillusion a kid.

"That's right, Billy, we're the real thing," I said with a straight face.

"Why?" asked Mike. "Are you doing a term paper on hippies or something?"

"No, nothing like that," replied Billy earnestly. "I like hippie stuff." He said it in a low voice, as if he might be overhead and immediately committed. It was like saying out loud that he liked to molest sheep or something.

"Far out!" I said, and he glowed to hear somebody actually speak hippie talk in his presence.

"What do you know about hippies?" asked Mike. "I mean, how did you hear about us?"

"I read all the magazines. There's been articles about hippies in Life and Time and even Reader's Digest. I've cut out every article I've found. And sometimes on TV they show hippies demonstrating or dancing or something. And I listen to the Beatles and even Bob Dylan, though I don't always understand all the words."

"No one does," Mike said. "That's the point."

"Why do you like hippies?" I asked.

"Oh, there's so cool! I hate this town. It's so dumb and backwards. I mean, you can't believe this place. It's as square as you can get. I think it would be so cool to grow my hair long and go to San Francisco and join a rock and roll band. But my mom won't even let me grow my hair so it touches my ears."

"Yeah, old people just don't understand, do they?" I said. "They want everybody to look the same."

Billy was beaming with joy to have someone agree with him, to understand his desire to be different. He needed so little to make him happy.

"Where are you guys from?" he asked.

"I'm from Haight-Ashbury," said Mike. "Brian's from the East Village."

"Oh, wow! No shit?" gasped Billy. I frowned at Mike.

"Hey, man," I said. "Billy's all right, dig it? We don't have to jive him, man; he's one of us. I'm from Ohio. Mike's from LA."

"Wow! You mean Los Angeles? Wow." Billy was easily impressed, but I could see he was thrilled to hear me say he was one of us.

"Are there other kids around here who think like you do?"

"Not many. Most of 'em are redneck crackers. They just want to ranch or sell used cars like their dads. But there's a few of us out at the JC. We get together and listen to cool records and wear headbands and stuff. Just in the room, you know? We'd get kicked out if anybody knew."

"Bold stuff," said Mike. "You ever get any good shit?"

"What?"

"You know. Shit. Dope. Weed. Smoke. Grass."

Billy's voice sank to a whisper. "You mean, like… pot?"

"Yeah. Or acid, hash, speed, anything?"

"Nah. Where would we get anything like that around here? Everybody just drinks Pearl or Lone Star. There's none of that stuff in Texas."

"Not around here?" Mike raved. "Why, my ignorant young friend, you are fortunate enough to be sitting in the middle of one of the best sources of *Lophophora williamsii* in the world."

"Huh?"

"Peyote, my boy, peyote. The food of the gods."

"Peyote? You mean that little cactus?"

"Exactly."

"You mean you can smoke peyote?"

"You don't smoke it, you eat it."

"With caution," I added. I had visions of an entire cell of novice hippies offing themselves on strychnine. "You shouldn't do it alone the first time."

"Really? Peyote? Shit, it grows everywhere around here!" Mike and I looked at each other.

"Really?" I asked. "Everywhere?"

"Oh, hell, yes. I got some out in my back yard."

"Then what," Mike asked me, "were we doing risking our necks out there by the river in CIA-controlled country?" I could only shrug.

"Wow, this is neat," said Billy. "Is that why you came here?"

"All the way from Boulder, Colorado," Mike answered. "Just so we could visit your pleasant little pokey here, as it turns out."

"Aw, Sheriff Delgado, he's okay. He'll treat you all right."

"He sure has so far. Compared to the way we've been living, this is a palace."

"Oh, yeah, that's the other thing I wanted to ask you. Is there anything I can get for you guys?"

"I'm afraid our resources are somewhat meager – even exhausted," said Mike with affected dignity.

"Oh, that's okay. I can get you some stuff."

"Well, I'd like something to read," I said. "A magazine or a paperback or something."

"I'd sure like some candy," added Mike. "Maybe some Hershey bars or a Twinkie?"

"Sure, I can do that. Anything else?"

"Yeah," said Mike. "Can you bring us some of that peyote out of your yard?"

"Yeah, sure," he said, obviously pleased to be helping our hippie endeavors. I think it never occurred to him that he could get into trouble smuggling drugs into jail. He left after some more conversation.

The boy was as good as his word. He returned in the morning with a full grocery bag. As usual, he simply walked into the jail. The bag was overflowing with reading materials and candy of all sorts. In the bottom were a half-dozen peyote cactus. He must have dug them up roots and all with a shovel. They looked like green lumpy carrots.

"My boy, you're a prince," said Mike.

Billy watched wide-eyed as we cleaned the peyote with our spoons and ate it. He looked as if he were watching us take the sacrament. Which we were, sort of. We chatted for hours with Billy as we munched the candy. He had to go to school before the buttons came on, but he promised to come back later. We assured him it would be all right if he brought some friends.

We spent that day in cosmic realms, totally unaffected by our surroundings. We felt safe and secure there. It really was a nice little jail. Certainly the best one I ever tripped in.

Billy came by to visit us during his lunch break from school. He brought his girl friend Alicia and another guy, Ron. I felt a little like a pet hippie in a zoo as he introduced us to his friends. He was clearly glorying in being so tight with two of our alien species.

I kept eyeing Alicia. She was really a good-looking girl and two days in the slammer was already working on my libido - what must it be like for lifers? I noticed that Ron was looking at her a lot, too. I thought she was aware of both of us and was enjoying the attention.

Mike as usual seemed to have no interest in anything on the physical plane.

We chatted with them for an hour, then they had to get back. Billy promised to visit again after school - with more candy, as we had finished the first load.

"Your friends are welcome again, if they want," I said, meaning Alicia of course. It didn't seem likely to lead anywhere, but we had managed to get just about everything else we wanted in that jail.

They all did visit us that evening. They told us about their lives. They all seemed fairly comfortable and well off. I suspected that most local kids didn't get a chance even at junior college. So these were Rio Grande City's best and brightest. And as usual, it is the people with leisure and no responsibilities who were interested in social change, not the ones who need it the most.

All three of them were bright and articulate, but their education was sorely lacking. I wrote out a truly eclectic reading list that included Hermann Hesse, Ken Kesey, Lenny Bruce, Eldridge Cleaver, Aldous Huxley, Baba Ram Dass (nee Richard Alpert), Bertrand Russell, Richard Farina, Kurt Vonnegut, and George Bernard Shaw. Mike gave them a discography of Jefferson Airplane, Velvet Underground, Bob Dylan, Leonard Cohen, Grateful Dead, and Donovan. We sent them back to their circle of Texas-avant-garde friends, bearing these seeds of subversion to carry throughout south Texas. We urged them to have the lists photocopied and posted on bulletin boards. We felt like a cross between union organizers and evangelists.

Billy drove to Laredo that same evening to a bookstore that carried some of those books and still somehow survived. It was exciting to be exposing these eager kids to the tenets of our lives and the kids were as thrilled as middle-aged virgins to be finally finding out what it was all about. They knew about headbands and bellbottoms, but they hadn't a clue about the philosophical basis of what the hippies were doing. By Wednesday they were cutting classes to attend our school for subversion.

We talked about the war, and Mike curdled their blood with a story or two of what the US was doing in Southeast Asia. He shocked them to their roots when he told them that America was fighting on the wrong side, supporting a tyrannical regime against the democratic will of its people. He laid on them some of his conspiracy theories, from the FBI killing JFK to the CIA-run cocaine trade in Latin America.

We explained about the military-industrial complex which Eisenhower had warned the country about, but which had since taken over every aspect of government, from foreign aggression to spying on and oppressing its own citizens; of reviving prohibition to jail anyone who wanted to be different, to be free.

We talked about the sexual revolution; how the pill had finally freed women from being in men's power; how hippies believed all races, nations, and genders were equal. We told them how the government was secretly thwarting civil rights legislation and enforcement, fanning the flames of racial hatred to keep its various oppressed peoples at each other's throats, unable to form an organized resistance.

We explained how the U.S was using a thousand times its fair share of the world's resources, knowingly poisoning the planet with toxics, nuclear waste, and atmospheric nuclear testing, all for immediate profits. We pointed out how the U.S supports its arms merchants by stirring up regional wars, then selling arms to both sides. We showed them the suicidal lunacy of the arms race.

Those three Texas kids absorbed all this in open-mouthed astonishment. They had never heard any one of these ideas, let alone all at once. It was like force-feeding them. We felt an urgency - after all, we only had three more days to convert them, to make them unwilling to serve their masters, to go out and proselytize in their turn. Who knows? Perhaps they could save the benighted state of Texas. Is this how Lenin felt in the Moscow train station?

Wednesday evening Sheriff Delgado brought us our dinner.

"You boys get ready tomorrow. I'm releasing you first thing in the morning."

"What?" I asked indignantly. "We're in till Friday evening."

"I don't care. I'm tired of feeding you. And I don't know what all you're telling those kids all day, but I think their parents will be happy to have you out of town, too."

"But our money hasn't come in yet," I said. "We can't leave town till it comes."

"That's not my problem, is it? You're on your own tomorrow morning."

"No way!" said Mike. "The judge gave us five days and we're doing five days. We know our rights."

"I'm telling you you're out!"

"Oh, yeah? What's the penalty for petty shoplifting in this town?"

"What? Why, it's a twenty-five dollar fine."

"Or five days in jail, huh? Our money should be here by then."

"Hey, wait a minute. Are you threatening…"

"I'm just saying it's going to be hard for us to stay in this town without any money."

The sheriff glared at us for a few minutes, considering.

"Thursday night," he growled. "No later."

"It's cold out there at night. Friday morning."

"Okay, okay! Friday morning."

"After breakfast."

"After breakfast!" He stormed out and slammed the door, rather maliciously, I thought, as it meant we couldn't watch M*A*S*H with his family that evening.

The next day we did what we could to complete the kids' course at the underground university. They were coming along well. I discussed Been Down So Long It Looks Like Up To Me with Billy and Alicia, while Mike and Ron compared and contrasted Gnossos Papadopoulos and the protagonist of Jimi Hendrix' Hey Joe.

When we told them we were being released in the morning they seemed crestfallen.

"What will you do? Where are you going?"

"Well, nowhere until our money arrives. Do you have any idea where we could stay for a few days, very inconspicuously? It doesn't have to be fancy. Just a roof over our heads."

"Hey, that gives me an idea," said Alicia. "Billy, what about the skating rink?"

"That is just a roof," said Ron.

"There's the office," said Billy. "At least it has walls."

"Skating rink?" I asked. "Sounds like a hard place to hide in."

"Naw, it's closed," said Billy. "A few years ago my old man tried to start a roller skating rink on some land he owned about a mile west of town. It's just a wood floor and a roof. It never really made it with the kids and it folded a year or two later."

"Does anybody ever go there?" Mike asked.

"Well, sometimes," Alicia said with a giggle and a look at Billy.

"Sometimes kids go there at night," said Billy with a shy grin. "There's this old mattress somebody hauled out there."

"I get the picture," I said. "And the office?"

"It's always locked. But I know where Dad keeps the key."

"That sounds great," I said. "How do we get there?"

"We can take you."

"Perfect. Can you pick us up in the morning?"

"Well, I suppose we better go to school. They might be getting suspicious that we've all been out sick all week. I can pick you up at lunch time."

So we were set. In the morning we took advantage of the showers and Mrs. Delgado's wonderful cooking one more time, then the sheriff released us. We thanked him and told him we would recommend his jail to all our friends.

Chapter Ten
Rollarama

At nine o'clock we were standing on the front steps of the Starr County courthouse, our sole belongings a fistful of one-dollar bills in my pocket. We walked to the Western Union office, in the back of the Chevy dealership, but our money still wasn't there. We laid low in a nearby highway culvert until noon, then returned to the courthouse. A few minutes later Billy and Alicia wheeled up in a big American car. We clambered in back and lay down on the seat as Billy took off. A few minutes later he pulled off the highway into a gravel parking lot.

The skating rink was a big sagging wood floor with a roof of steel trusses and corrugated iron. Across the front gable we could just make out the faded words "Rio Grande Rollarama". An eight-by-eight office in the front left corner had a plank or two missing from the walls. A door stood chained and padlocked under a sign that said "Tickets" in olde west lettering.

Billy pulled a rusted key out of his jeans and unlocked the door. The inside was dark and musty and the floor was littered with trash and rat droppings.

"I love what you've done with the place," Mike said. Billy looked embarrassed.

"It's fine," I reassured him.

"You sure? It's kinda messy."

"Sure, we've been in worse places than this. It's only another day or two."

"We've got to get back to school," said Alicia. "We'll come visit you tonight, okay?"

"That'd be great. Thanks a lot."

Mike found an old broom and we swept the floor. I checked out the mattress to see if we wanted to bring it in, but it was filthy and vermin-infested. Those kids must be desperate to screw on that thing. We found a roll of canvas awning material and made a rough bed out of that. Then we got loaded and hung out. At dusk I walked to a little market and bought two cans of refried beans and a pile of tortillas. Four dinners for under a dollar. It made me nervous walking on the highway. I kept having images from Easy Rider of a shotgun coming out the window of a passing truck. But no one hassled me except for one beer can thrown at my head and another truck that swerved off the road at me. They didn't seem to be serious murder attempts, so I figured it was just normal South Texas boys fooling around.

Mike and I had dinner cold, then did two more of Billy's buttons. We got nervous about somebody coming by to screw and finding us there. We didn't like the idea of being trapped in that office with only one door, so we climbed up into the rafters above the rink. It was actually quite comfortable up there. We were still there an hour or two later when Billy, Alicia, and Ron showed up. They climbed up to join us. There in the darkness we initiated them in the joys of good hashish. They loved it, and we spent the entire evening giggling like children.

It was great fun, but it was also an important part of their education. First, of course, it was an integral ritual of the culture: the ceremonial filling and lighting of the bowl; the fraternal passing of the warm, glowing pipe; and above all the drug rap, detailing the lore, history, and probable source of the drug and anecdotes about memorable characters and experiences on hash.

Secondly, it was good for them to get stoned, to see that being stoned is just plain good fun, relaxed and comfortable, and instantly giving the lie to all the propaganda they'd been taught over the years. Once is enough to convince you that the authorities have been bullshitting you all along. And if they lied about that, what else are they lying about?

And third and perhaps most important, it gave them a chance to see us stoned. When you get stoned with someone, it is impossible to remain cool in the negative sense. You do all the silly, embarrassing things everyone else does - transpose words, forget what you were saying, and laugh helplessly at absurdities. Those kids saw us as we really were - not super-hip dudes from some unattainable, alien world, but just two kids a year or two older than they who had had some different experiences that had changed them.

It was an evening of laughter and friendship and I think we all felt as close as family when they at last climbed down to go home. I gave Billy a few simple tests to assure myself that he could drive safely, then we gave them the traditional hippie bear hug and sent them back to their parents. Mike and I felt so good as they drove off that we did another couple of buttons to celebrate. We had a beautiful trip and saw a gorgeous desert sunrise before we crashed.

The next day was Saturday, and we had pinned our hopes on our money arriving that day. Mike, as the least conspicuous, walked into town in late afternoon and checked at the Chevy dealership. Still no money. He thought perhaps it had somehow been delivered to the jail by mistake and went over to the courthouse. Sheriff Delgado was not pleased to see him again and threatened to run him out of town, but he did say the money hadn't come there. Mike walked back dejected. We knew it was only a matter of time before somebody hostile spotted us and kicked the shit out of us. It's just what you did if you were a redneck and something came by you didn't understand.

We didn't see the kids all day Saturday and assumed they were absorbing their experience of the night before. We had dinner and climbed up into the rafters when it got dark. It turned out to be a good idea.

Saturday night in Rio Grande City is party night. The old folks go to the country western bar to drink, dance, and fight. The kids pay drunks to buy them six-packs of Pearl and Lone Star at the package store, then hang out at the Range Burger Drive-Inn at the east end of town, sitting on hoods and talking loud. Then they jump into their cars or pickups and peel out, their tires screeching and smoking as they tear through town, hell-bent for action. The only problem is that there's no place to drive to. So they roar out of town to the skating rink, turn around, and roar back to the drive-in, just as if they'd really been somewhere. It's pathetic, but what can you do if you live in a place like Rio Grande City?

All this made for a lot of commotion out at the rink. Every half hour or so a carload of drunk and rowdy rednecks would blast in, toss a few empties into the skating rink, then peel out, spraying gravel across the rink as they fishtailed back onto the highway. Each time disturbed our stoned repose and filled us with paranoid delusions about being lynched or raped or both.

Around midnight a car skidded in and stopped and a figure leaped out and raced into the rink below us. We froze, holding our breaths.

"Guys? Are you up there?" It was Ron.

"Over here, man. What's up?"

"You gotta help me. I'm in deep trouble." His voice was trembling. He was scared.

"Hey, calm down, brother. Come on up."

He swung up beside us. Even in the dark we could see his eyes wide and white.

"What's going down?"

"It's Billy. He's out to kill me."

"Billy? No way, man. You guys are best friends."

"Not any more. He had a date with Alicia tonight, but she called him to say she was sick and couldn't go out. He couldn't reach me, so he went out with some buddies to go drinking."

"So?"

"So after a few hours he heads up to the burger place to get something to eat and he runs into a friend of ours, Jimmie. Jimmie isn't all that bright. He says, 'Hey Billy, where were Alicia and Ron going earlier tonight? I saw them heading out of town in Ron's car.'"

"Oh, Ron," said Mike. "Are you diddling Billy's girl?"

"No! Well, uh, sort of. But she's not his girl, not really. I mean, they've been dating, but she's not wearing his ring or anything."

"But people think they're together, right? Or Jimmy wouldn't have asked Billy about it."

"Well, yeah, I guess so."

"And Billy thinks she's his girl, right?"

"Oh, yeah. He thinks he's in love."

"Oh, Ron," said Mike again. "We are disappointed in you. He's your best friend."

"I know. I feel terrible about it, but I just couldn't help it. You know how Alicia is. She's so friendly and nice, and so darn good looking."

"She's a sexy woman," I agreed. "I'd jump on in a minute."

"Yeah, exactly. Well, it was her idea. I mean, she suggested telling him she was sick and all. I didn't like it, but I wanted her so bad and I figured he'd never find out."

"Tell me," I said. "Was it worth it?"

His eyes lit up. "Oh, yeah," he said dreamily. "It was great. She's great. Her tits are like…"

"Please," I begged. "A gentleman never discusses a lady he's bedded. It shows disrespect. Besides, I'm horny enough as it is."

"But what about Billy? Jimmy told me he went to get his gun."

"No shit? Do you think he'd use it?"

"I don't know. If he's mad enough, I think he might. He's got quite a temper."

"What does Alicia say about it? Does she love you?"

"She says she likes both of us. She likes Billy but doesn't want to go steady with anybody right now. She says she's not ready for that yet."

"A wise decision," said Mike. "You're all too young to be making commitments that could tie you up the rest of your lives. You've got to live some life before you know what you want out of it."

"I may not have a life after tonight. What am I gonna do?"

"Where's Alicia?" I asked.

"At her house. She had to be home by midnight."

"Does she know Billy knows?"

"No. I met Jimmy at the drive-in after I took her home."

"She should know about it," Mike said.

"She's got her own phone in her room."

"Good. Call her and tell her about it. Tell her to stay there."

"Okay. What about Billy?"

"My guess," I said, "is that he'll come here when he can't find you anyplace else."

"Oh, shit. You're probably right. What can I do?"

"If I were you I'd stay out of Billy's sight until he calms down. Go out a long way away and drive around or something. Don't go home yet. Can you get away with that?"

"Yeah, my parents never know when I come home."

"Good. Come back here at say, five o'clock and we'll talk again."

"Okay. And thanks."

He took off, spraying yet more gravel across the floor of the skating rink. We watched his tail lights disappear in the distance.

"You think Billy'd shoot him?" I asked Mike.

"I think he'd want to shoot him. I don't think he'd really do it. But you never know when testosterone is involved."

"I know. I hope he shows up here so we can talk to him. Damn!" I shifted uncomfortably.

"You okay?"

"Yeah. I've just got these two regrets. One is that I wish I'd known she was ready to drop Billy. I would have made a move on her myself."

"And the other?"

"I wish I had let Ron describe her tits."

"You're the slave of your gonads, just like Billy. To be truly spiritual you have to rise above the physical."

"If I thought I had to give up sex to reach nirvana, I'd give up religion instead."

"But sex ties us to our animal bodies."

"I like being tied to my animal body. I believe we are animal bodies, with animal brains. We use our brains to try to make sense of the world and that leads to religion, the desire to understand the world. I have no idea yet what it's all about. Maybe nothing. But for me personally, I don't think it involves separating our minds from our bodies. That's dualism, and it's exactly what's wrong with the world."

"Materialism is what's wrong with the world - people thinking that acquiring material things is the goal and the justification for anything they do."

"But that doesn't mean that material things are meaningless or evil. If a man steals, it's not the gold that's at fault. If he rapes, it's not his testicles that are wrong. In both cases it's his lack of respect for his fellow beings. It's his dualism that allows him to put himself on one side, and to put other people and their possessions and interests on the other. He thinks that other people aren't like him, that their feelings aren't as important as his. If he realized that we're all related, he wouldn't do it."

"That's simplistic. If you…"

Just then a car skidded into the lot and Billy ran into the rink. He was carrying a gun.

"Brian! Mike! Are you here?"

"Yeah, we're here, Billy. Come on up."

"I'm looking for Ron. Have you seen him?"

"He was here earlier."

"He was? Where did he go?"

"Out of town. A long way out of town."

"Shit." He stood there a moment, trying to decide what to do. "Well, he has to come back sometime. I'm going to wait at his house." He started back to his car.

"Billy, wait," I shouted after him. "We told him to come back here later."

"You did?"

"Yeah. So there's no point in your going looking for him. You can stay here with us and wait for him."

He looked undecided. Clearly he wanted to go do something now, not sit and wait.

"Come on, man," said Mike. "Have a smoke with us."

Finally Billy shoved the gun into his belt and swung up into the rafters. He was shaking and his shirt was soaked with sweat. I eyed the gun uneasily as he settled down.

"So, Billy," I said. "You're looking for Ron?"

"I sure as hell am! Do you know what that fucker did?"

"Yeah. He told us."

"Shit! Is he bragging about it already?"

"No, but he knows you're looking for him, and he's scared."

"He's as scared as you are right now," added Mike.

"Scared? I'm not scared. I'm mad. Mad enough to kill the bastard."

"Don't tell me you're not scared," said Mike. "I was in Nam. I can smell it in your sweat. You're afraid of what's going to happen when you meet Ron. You're afraid you might not have the nerve to do it, or maybe that you will."

"If you're like me," I said, "the scariest thing is feeling trapped. Like there's no way out. You can't see how tomorrow can arrive unless you've either killed Ron or you've chickened out. And either one is too terrible to imagine. Either you're a murderer facing ten to twenty years of getting screwed in the butt in Huntsville; or you've shown yourself and everyone else that you're not a man; that you've lost your girl, your guts, and your pride all in one night. Pretty grim."

Billy's eyes got even wider, then he turned away.

"That's it, isn't it?" I persisted. "Sure, you're mad as hell. You've been hurt, and hurt bad. You've been betrayed by both your girl and your best friend, and it seems like you've lost them both. But even more than all that anger and hurt, you're feeling trapped and alone and scared."

"You're not alone, Billy," said Mike. "We're your friends. We love you."

Billy shuddered, fighting his emotions. I thought he was trying not to cry, but then he turned and snarled at us.

"Fuck you! What do you know about it? What do you care? You're not from around here. Easy for you to spout off with your free advice. Tomorrow or the next day you'll be gone, and I'll still be here. I have to live in this town. Am I just supposed to go to school on Monday and say, 'Hi Ron. Hi Alicia. Did you guys have a nice time fucking Saturday night?' She lied to me! She's my girl!"

"She's not anybody's girl," said Mike. "She's her own woman. She makes up her own mind who she wants to be with."

"She wants to be with me!" he screamed.

"Well, she obviously likes you, Billy," I said calmly. "She's been going out with you a lot. But from what I hear, no promises have been made."

"I was going to ask her to go steady. Soon. I was going to ask her to marry me."

"I don't think she's ready for that, Billy. I don't think it's you. I think she's just not ready to settle down yet."

"What do you know about it?"

"A woman waiting for a man to ask her to marry him doesn't go out with his best friend. Ron didn't drag her off by the hair, you know. She went willingly. She's got a right to do that."

"But with Ron? That's what really pisses me off. If it'd been somebody else I'd just be at home feeling heartbroken. But he's my buddy. We do everything together."

"I'll say," said Mike. I shot him a dirty look, but I don't think Billy caught the comment.

"But he and Alicia are friends, too," I said. "They know and like each other and they're both attractive and healthy. It's a natural thing to happen."

"That doesn't make it right."

"No, it doesn't," said Mike, turning to me. "Billy's right. It wasn't just boy meets girl, boy mounts girl. They both knew it would hurt Billy. And they did it anyway."

"But if they wanted each other, which they clearly did, anything they did would hurt Billy. Billy wants Alicia all to himself, and obviously that's not what she wants. So there's hurting in the wind for Billy no matter what. It would have been cooler for her to break it off with Billy before starting anything with Ron."

"Yeah," said Billy. "If she had talked to me first, told me she wasn't interested in me anymore."

"What would you have felt?"

"Well, I would have been upset, sure. I love her."

"And if you'd found out later she was seeing Ron?"

"I'd have punched his lights out!"

"Right. So this way is no different. You just took the one-two punch all at once."

"A three punch, so to speak," said Mike.

"But she lied to me!"

"Yeah, that's hard to take, too. And that's wrong of her. But look at it from her side. She likes you, but she wanted Ron too. She couldn't just say 'Look, I want to go out with Ron.' You wouldn't have let it happen. So she probably felt she had no other choice. If you hadn't been so possessive, maybe she wouldn't have felt that way. Maybe that's just what drove her to see someone else. It wouldn't be the first time that someone has chosen that way to send a good clear message to someone who doesn't want to get the message. You might do the same thing if you were seeing a girl and she was getting way too serious for you. Wouldn't you?"

Billy thought about this for a while, and I could see he was calming down a little. But then he flared up again.

"But what about Ron? He knows how I feel about Alicia, and he did it anyway."

"Men are simpler creatures," said Mike. "They tend to think with their cocks."

"Inelegantly but accurately put," I agreed. "Again, put yourself in his place. You know how attractive Alicia is, how she makes you want her. I sure do. Mike would too, if his balls hadn't been eaten off by creeping Oriental religions. Say she'd been Ron's girl all along. He's your buddy; you hang out together, so you're around her a lot. The desire builds up so it's there all the time, so it's hard to be around her."

"Now who's being inelegant?" put in Mike.

"Difficult to be around her. What's more, you get the sense from her that the feeling's mutual, that she's attracted to you. That's one of the best feelings around; when you realize that somebody that turns you on is just as hot for you. If she were alone you'd be on her in a flash. But you think, 'I can't make a move on her. She's Ron's girl.' But then she comes on to you. She suggests it. She tells you she wants to make it with you. Now you tell me the truth. What would you do?"

"The truth now, not the bible school answer," said Mike.

Billy thought for while, then looked up with a crooked smile. "I'd probably take her up on it and hope he never found out."

"Wonderful things, testicles," said Mike. "So charmingly predictable."

"So now you want to kill either Alicia or Ron for doing just what you probably would have done in their place."

"Doesn't seem right, does it, Billy?" said Mike. "If Ron had met Alicia first, it'd be you driving around out there scared shitless that your best friend was going to kill you."

"Killing him would fuck up all three of your lives forever," I said. "It sure as hell wouldn't get Alicia back and you'd have lost your best friend. Ron would be dead, you'd be in the pen, and Alicia would have to live with that guilt forever. That's not revenge, Billy, that's a waste of three good people."

"Yeah," said Mike. "The world is short of good people. We can't afford to go around killing each other off. Violence isn't the way. Violence causes violence. Look at Jesus and Gandhi and Martin Luther King. They were successful. They got things done. Not by blowing away people that pissed them off. But by trying to understand them, putting themselves in their place."

"What am I supposed to do?" Billy wailed. "Just forget it? Pretend it didn't happen? I can't do that. As far as I'm concerned, they can both just kiss my ass."

"Well, that's one way of turning the other cheek," I said, "but I don't think that's what Jesus meant." Billy snorted at that.

"But you're right," I went on. "This is a big hurt, the kind grown-ups get. You'll probably never forget this much pain. You want to strike back against the pain. But it's the hurt feelings and the resentment and the anger and jealousy that you need to battle, not Alicia and Ron."

"Hurting them back really won't make you feel better," added Mike. "Believe me. You'd regret it the instant you did it."

"The only thing you can do is to forgive them. They hurt you, sure, but they were only being human, doing what humans do. Having feelings means they get hurt sometimes. Maybe you can't be friends with them anymore, and that would be a real shame. But it's better than blowing your lives to pieces."

"And maybe you can be friends again sometime," said Mike. "It's up to the three of you."

Billy sat for a long while. We let him think. After a long time he turned and looked at us.

"I'm going home," he said. "Tell Ron not to worry. I'm not going to come after him." He swung down to the floor and walked slowly back to his car, looking like the saddest, most hurting person in the world. He drove off into the first tints of dawn.

Mike and I looked at each other in the half-light. "I think we did it," I said.

"I think so," Mike agreed. "I was trying so hard to say the one thing that might get through. I guess one of us must have found it."

"I think we just showed him that there's another way. The Code of the West says you have to have a gunfight on Main Street. But Billy's smart enough to see the other sides. I think he's going to be all right."

Ron drove up a few minutes later. "I got here a little while ago and saw Billy's car," he said. "So I stayed out of sight. I was scared to come in."

"It's okay, Ron. He's not gunning for you," said Mike. "But he hurts like a son of a bitch. He feels like you kicked him in the balls and he's never done anything to deserve it."

Ron hung his head. "I know. It's true. All night long I've been driving around out there, thinking about how he must feel. I feel pretty shitty myself. I don't know what I was thinking. I guess I just hoped he wouldn't ever find out. I was just thinking about Alicia."

"We know. And Billy understands that too. But it still hurts. You've probably lost him as a friend, and that's a real shame. But maybe not. You're going to have to give him some time. I'd leave him alone unless he approaches you."

"And I'd keep the thing with Alicia invisible. Or better yet, forget it for a while. No need to rub his nose in it."

"Yeah, I talked to Alicia, and she feels rotten too. We agreed we made a mistake. She wanted to call him right away to apologize."

"I'd tell her to give him today to himself, then do that tonight. I think he'd be glad to hear from her, especially with an apology."

"Go on home now, Ron. And get back on that reading list."

"Okay." He shuffled his feet uncomfortably. "Look, I don't know what you guys said to Billy tonight, but thanks. I didn't think anything could stop him from coming after me. I thought I was dead, and deserved it."

"No one deserves to be dead, Ron," said Mike. "It's the hippie creed." We both gave him long hugs, then he drove off.

"I wonder if Alicia will need our counseling too," I said.

"You stay away from her," said Mike. "Billy's still got that gun."

"Don't worry. Man, I'm tired. I think I'm finally coming down from the peyote."

"Yeah, I guess so. Quite a trip, huh?"

We dragged ourselves into the shack to crash and slept till the afternoon.

When we woke up I walked into town to the Western Union office. My money order was there, but not Mike's. I cashed it at the gas station and walked back.

I told Mike I was anxious to get up to Fort Worth and find out what had happened to Elissa and my stuff. Mike said he had no interest in going to Fort Worth. He'd had enough of Texas. He planned to go straight to LA when his money arrived.

There didn't seem to be any reason for me to hang around. I gave Mike a few bucks to keep him going, and then we gave each other the hippie hug. I had nothing to pack, so we just went out to the highway and I started walking. A car flashed past a few minutes later and I turned to thumb. Mike was already out of sight. I walked almost eight miles before an old couple in a Nash Rambler picked me up.

Chapter Eleven
Lousy Hitchhiking

The old couple never spoke to me for the two-hour drive to Laredo. I wondered if they were frightened by my long hair and ragged clothes, my Indian-print headband, the paisley patches on my bell-bottoms. Maybe they picked me up before they got a good look at me. Perhaps they were just kind and quiet people who couldn't think of anything to say to such a bizarre and alien being. At any rate, they dropped me off at a truck stop on the outskirts of Laredo where I would have a better chance of catching a ride north. I lingered over lunch at the diner and checked out the truck drivers. They were hard looking men in dirty cowboy hats and pointed-toe boots. They looked pretty much like the other cowboys and ranch hands I'd seen all over south Texas. The only way I could tell they were truck drivers was that only their left arms were sunburned. I approached several for a ride. Most just looked me over and told me to fuck off. The afternoon was wearing on before one agreed to give me a lift. He was only going as far as San Antonio, then heading west to Tucson, but I figured it was better to be moving than not. I had heard San Antonio had a small hippie scene. Maybe I could find a crash pad there and get a ride with some hippies.

We went out to his truck and climbed in. I was pleased I at least knew how to climb up into the cab. It's not easy if you haven't done it before. I had only been in a big rig once before, years ago in Ohio on one of my very first times hitchhiking. It had been raining and I was cold and scared and I was thrilled that this huge truck had ground to a stop for me. I felt like a real hobo, riding in an eighteen-wheeler. I'd looked up at that huge wall of metal in confusion. Then I noticed the steps let into the side and scrambled on up. I made use of the convenient big shiny silver handle that runs up just behind the passenger door, only to discover it was the exhaust pipe and that I had burned all the skin off the palm of my hand. I'd been too shocked and embarrassed to make a fuss, so I squeezed my hand between my knees and tried not to moan for the whole ride from Xenia to Columbus.

This time I swung myself into the seat as if I knew what I was doing. In a minute we were off, cranking up through what seemed like dozens of gears. The guy was friendly enough, and we chatted as we roared north on I-35. He told me he was running a load of appliances from Brownsville to Tucson. He asked me where I was from and what I was doing, and I tried to tell the truth as much as I could without mentioning drugs, politics, Vietnam, religion, or my impressions of Texas and its inhabitants. That left food, sex, and music, but that was enough to fill up the three hours to San Antonio. Actually, I was enjoying riding in the big comfortable cab, and I began to consider asking if I could ride with him to Tucson. This whole trip had started out as a trip to the coast, after all, and Tucson was a hell of a lot closer to California than Fort Worth was. But I wanted my stuff back and I wanted to see Elissa again, so when we got to the intersection with I-10, he pulled over and I thanked him and climbed down. He roared off in a blinding cloud of dust and flying gravel and I turned my back and covered my face until it cleared. Then I looked around. It was not an encouraging sight.

I had imagined the intersection of the interstates to be in downtown San Antonio. It's one of the main crossroads in the whole country. I-35 runs from the border at Laredo all the way up to Minnesota, while I-10 runs from Jacksonville to Los Angeles. I thought it would be a busy place crowded with truck stops and restaurants and a relatively easy place to catch a ride. But there's a beltway around San Antonio to carry all that heavy traffic around the city. I was standing at a cloverleaf in the middle of the Texas plains, as flat as a griddle, with not so much as a building in sight in any direction. There was little traffic coming up from Laredo and even less on the beltway road. A car or truck passed maybe every ten minutes, going ninety or more, bent on getting where they were going and not at all inclined to stop for some scruffy figure standing out there in the middle of the plains without so much as a suitcase. Car after car whipped past with no thought of stopping. Sometimes I saw faces staring out at me: bored salesmen dazed from hours of driving through featureless scrub land; wide-eyed children with their foreheads pressed against the glass; frightened-looking women no doubt thinking that there was no amount of money they would take to stop out there and let me get in the car with them. They were probably wondering what the hell I was doing out here all by myself, and imagining terrible stories to account for me.

The afternoon light faded and the sun sank toward the western rim of this immense table I was standing on. A line of clouds like the edge of a blanket came up from the west until the sky was covered. It began to get cold. I was only 150 miles from Mexico; I had imagined it would be hot here. But it was now late February, and it gets bitterly cold in the winter in Texas, even down here. All I had to wear was the jeans and shirt I had on, an old Navy surplus pea coat with the sleeves falling off, and an olive drab plastic poncho I had found in a trash bin in Rio Grande City. I took the poncho out of my pocket and pulled it over my head. It was thin plastic and it didn't close up on the sides, so it just flapped in the breeze when a car zipped by. I realized that it wasn't going to keep me warm at all and the temperature was quickly falling. If I didn't get a ride before dark I could be in serious trouble. Normally if I get stuck hitching I'll start walking, as much for the feeling of making progress as any real hope of finding a better spot. But I could see the road for miles ahead and there was no hint of a gas station or phone, much less someplace warm to sleep. This was a lousy place to hitchhike — you normally want a stoplight or a fast food place to make people stop and take a look at you. But at least the cars turning onto the beltway had to slow down to take the cloverleaf. Out there on the open road there was even less chance that somebody would stop. Also, there was an overpass there that could conceivably offer some protection and there was clearly no other scrap of shelter this side of the horizon in any direction. So there was no point in trying to go anywhere. There was nothing to do but stand there till I get a ride.

As the last light faded, my chances and my spirits dropped. At least in daylight they could see me standing there for a long time and it gave them some time to consider picking me up. At night, their lights didn't pick me up until they were right next to me. They just got a quick glimpse of some dark hooded figure standing out there in the dark. By the time they did wonder if I might be a hitchhiker, they were two miles down the road. It was basically hopeless, I realized, but I couldn't think of anything else to do.

There was a big green highway sign there marking the exit, the kind you see hundreds of times a day without thinking. Out of boredom, I walked over to examine it more closely. It was really quite large, with two heavy square wooden posts set deeply in the ground. The letters were raised pieces of white metal, fastened onto the green sign. Little circular reflectors fit into round holes in the letters. I was struck by how much work went into designing, building, and erecting this one dinky little sign. One letter was loose, so I pried it up further and pulled out two or three of the reflectors.

With the darkness came a wind. It wasn't blowing hard, but it was really cold and it cut through my thin clothes as if I were naked. I hunkered down in the slight shelter of a clump of mesquite, wrapped the poncho tightly around my knees, and felt sorry for myself. Every half-hour or so a light blinked on the southern horizon and I watched the car approach, trying to decide if it was worth getting up to thumb. In the end, of course, I couldn't afford to let even a tiny chance of a ride go by, so I struggled to my feet, shook the kinks out of my knees, and walked over to the edge of the pavement. Clutching the poncho around me, I stuck out my thumb and put on my most ingratiating non-threatening face. I held a reflector and tried to flash it toward the car to let them know I was there. It seemed to take hours for the car to get there, and then it was upon me in seconds. It flashed past with a Doppler roar, whipping my poncho from my grasp to flutter over my head and let out what little warm air I'd managed to collect. Sometimes the drivers, startled by my sudden appearance, jerked the wheel in surprise and the car lurched into the left lane. Not one touched a brake. I returned to my bush and squatted down out of the wind again.

I'd been miserable for a long time, but now I was starting to get scared. It was completely dark, with an overcast sky. There was no chance of catching a ride until daylight. I had no idea what time it was, but it'd been dark maybe two or three hours, so it couldn't be much after eight or nine. At this time of year it wouldn't be light until six or seven. That meant I was going to have to last ten or eleven hours. It was getting colder fast. When a car went past I could see my breath in the glare of the lights. It couldn't be much above forty and bound to get colder as the night went on. There was a real chance I could die of exposure out there. I had no food, no water, nothing to make a fire with. I couldn't think of a thing to do to help myself.

As it got later, the sparse traffic died away. I waited for an hour and only one car appeared, going south. There was no point in standing up there in the wind, so I started walking toward the overpass.

I'd noticed that many overpasses have a ledge up underneath the ends of the bridge where I could at least get out of the wind. Maybe I could roll up in the poncho like a burrito. It was so dark it was hard to walk on the sloping gravel on the berm, so I got on the pavement and walked right down the middle of the interstate. It was a mile or more to the overpass and it seemed like I'd been walking a long time when I made out the guardrails of the bridge looming up ahead. I held onto the concrete wall and let my feet slide down the steep bank. I slithered down through some thorny shrubs and managed to catch myself before reaching the edge of the road cut below. The ground under the bridge was a steep slope of concrete at nearly a 45-degree angle. To my dismay, there was no ledge at the top. The slope just came up to a wall maybe two feet high that abutted the bottom of the bridge. I went down the slope and crossed the other highway in hopes there was something better on the other side, but it was the same. I scrambled around in the bushes beside the road, hoping there was some kind of a cavity I could crawl into, but there was nothing. In the end, I decided that the wind was less at the top of the slope, just under the bridge. I duck-walked out to the middle of the slope and crouched there with my back against the wall, the top of my head against the bridge, and tried to brace my feet on the steep slope. It was covered with that fine gray dust that seems to blanket everything near a highway. I brushed away as much as I could with my hands, but it was still slippery. I pulled the poncho around me and tucked it between my feet to hold it down. Then I sat, wishing with all my might that I were someplace else. What I wouldn't give for even a nice warm jail cell now.

Several times during that interminable night I heard a car approaching on I-35. I huddled there, too miserable to get up and clamber up to the bridge to thumb. When the car at last thundered over my head I had to wonder if that wasn't the one car on the whole road from Laramie to Duluth that would have picked me up. It was probably three love-starved college girls from Laredo looking to find some wandering hippie to introduce them to the joys of sex. But even these thoughts couldn't keep me warm for long. It was bone-chillingly cold now. I gripped the edges of the poncho to keep them closed and wrapped my arms around my knees to wait.

Even as exhausted as I was, it was almost impossible to get to sleep. Once or twice I dozed off, only to be awakened when a big rig thundered by right above my head. A couple of times I crawled out to look around or take a pee and there was nothing at all to see. The sky was flat black, the land flat to the horizon. There was no traffic. The only object to be seen on the whole plain was the hump of this overpass. Miserably, I crawled back in and tried to lock my feet against the concrete so I wouldn't slide down. In spite of my best efforts, however, I steadily skidded down the steep hill, a few inches every time I shifted my weight.

Sometime during the night I woke up and discovered I was wet. My breath condensing inside the poncho had soaked my clothes. Dark streaks of water ran down the slope from under the edge of the poncho. I was shivering violently and couldn't seem to stop. I knew I was bordering on hypothermia. Deciding I had to walk around to get my circulation going. I unlocked my frozen limbs and crept out from under the bridge. The ground was white. I bent down to feel it. There was a thin dusting of snow, dry and powdery, gathered in little heaps around the bases of the bushes. I was reminded of that famous Jack London short story, *To Build a Fire*, where a prospector is lost from his dog team in Alaska in the winter. He tries everything he can think of to stay alive, but he can't get a fire started and he eventually freezes to death. These conditions weren't anything like Alaska, but it was obviously a dangerous situation. I decided it was better to keep walking than to fall asleep again and possibly freeze. There was no place to walk to, so I shuffled across the bridge and back, once, twice. At least the wind had stopped. The snow swirled around my feet as I trudged along, beating my arms around my chest to stay warm. I noticed depressing little bits of flotsam beside the road: cigarette butts, gum wrappers, a broken tail light reflector. Never had a night been so long. After a few dozen times across the bridge, I couldn't face another one. I crawled back under the bridge, picked a dry spot, and locked myself into position again. I looked down the slope at the black pavement below. If I were to pass out, I'd tumble down the slope and roll right out onto the pavement. If a car came by, they would be unlikely to see me before they ran over me. With these cheerful thoughts for company, I fell asleep again.

When I woke up there was a change in the air — a slight breeze, a smell of something different. With a groan, I unlocked my stiff legs again and crawled out. It was time for more walking. When I pulled myself up onto the bridge, I could see the road stretching off into the distance in four directions. I finally realized that that meant that it was getting light. There was no welcoming glow of sun, no twittering of the dawn chorus, but there was a dim gray light filtering down from the overcast sky. I'd survived the night.

I had to get warm, so I started walking briskly north. There wasn't much hope of getting anywhere on foot, but there hadn't been a car in hours and I had to feel like I was doing something. I walked perhaps two or three miles, my mind so sluggish with the cold and my misery that I was hardly thinking at all. Suddenly I became aware of a sound behind me. I turned and looked back and saw a car bearing down on me. I stepped quickly off the road, dug a reflector out of my pocket, and waggled it at the car's lights. A rusty old Ford stake bed truck slowed and the driver looked me over as he went by. I turned and started walking again. A few hundred yards up the road, the truck swerved off onto the gravel and skidded to a stop.

My heart leaped with joy and I wanted to dash after it, but I was too cold and stiff to run. Also, in the past I'd several times had cars stop well past me, then when I ran to them they tore off with a hillbilly laugh and a spray of gravel in my face. I didn't think I could stand that right now, so I just kept up my pace. The truck didn't move. I could see the driver eyeing me in the rear view mirror as I approached. I came up to the passenger door. It was locked. The driver shouted at me through the glass.

"Where you going, son?" he called.

"Originally I was headed for Fort Worth," I shouted back. "Now I just want to go someplace warm."

He looked at me a moment more, then leaned across and unlocked the door. I clambered in and stammered out my thanks. He took off with a roar, and then looked over at me.

"How long you been out there anyway?" he asked.

"Too long. Most of yesterday and all night."

"You need to cut that hair," he said. "Nobody's going to pick you up in Texas with you looking like that."

Normally a comment like that would send me off on my canned tirade about freedom of expression and the founding fathers having long hair and so on, but right then I was too happy to be sitting in front of his blasting heater.

"Yeah, I figured that out eventually," I mumbled contritely. Nothing more was said. My clothes were steaming in the heat of the cab.

After an hour of driving we came to a roadside restaurant and stopped. He asked if I needed money, but I told him I had a bit. I had a big meal of bacon and eggs and hash browns and cup after cup of hot coffee. Finally I felt recovered enough to talk. We chatted and listened to country music for six more hours as we drove north across some of the most boring and uninviting country I'd ever seen.

Then a silhouette appeared on the horizon ahead, something tall and irregular. Finally I realized it was the skyline of Dallas, with skyscrapers standing out in the middle of the scrub brush. The driver was continuing north and had planned to take I-35 right through Dallas, but he took a small detour on I-35 West to take me to Fort Worth. Soon another, more humble skyline appeared ahead. The interstate bypassed around Fort Worth, and I asked him to let me out at a railroad switching area that appeared to be the closest approach to the city. I thanked him profusely and he drove away. I climbed down to the tracks and started walking toward Fort Worth. Fully recovered from my night on the plains, I was feeling pretty good. I liked coming into a new city like this: not knowing a soul, knowing nothing about the town, nobody knowing me. There wasn't a person on Earth who knew where I was right now. I was free to do anything I wanted, open to any adventure.

I realized it was still further away than I thought. Like the Emerald City, it seemed to always be the same distance away. I walked for a couple of hours, always hoping a slow freight would come by that I could jump into town, but none ever did. It was late afternoon before I came to a fairly ugly industrial area on the edge of town. I made my way through it, found a major road, and followed it into town. For lack of any better idea, I walked toward the biggest buildings, thinking that might be where the hippies and street people congregated. It was almost evening before I found myself on the streets of Fort Worth.

Chapter Twelve
The Cellar

It was a bigger city than I had imagined, looking a bit faded and old, but with a lot of new construction going on. I got something to eat at a greasy spoon diner and wondered how in the world I was going to find Elissa, if she was even here. Normally you can just walk around a city until you see some other longhairs, then ask them where you can crash. I tried that for a while but didn't see any. It was rush hour on a weekday, and everyone on the street was either a businessman or a woman shopping. They eyed my filthy disheveled appearance with curiosity mingled with distrust. I sure couldn't walk up to one of these suits and ask where hippies go to crash. It began to get dark, and I thought I might have to try to find a cheap hotel. Then I spotted two young guys and a girl across the street. They weren't dressed all that weird — they'd be picked as country cow freaks in New York or LA — but they all had hair and the girl was wearing granny glasses. I jaywalked across the street to catch them.

"Hey, brothers," I called out. "Know where I can crash tonight?"

They all turned to look at me in surprise. I must have made quite an impressive figure, with long greasy hair down to my shoulder blades, dirty clothes, and a mud-streaked plastic poncho, but they waited for me to catch up.

"Man, where are you from?" one of the guys asked, with a tone as if he wouldn't be surprised if I answered with something extraterrestrial.

"Well, right now I'm coming from the border and heading roughly toward San Francisco. But I have had a very rough trip and I just need a warm place to sleep. I've had it with sleeping outside."

I glanced at the girl to see if she was suitably impressed with my wild tale, but she was looking me over as if she had found me washed up on a beach.

"Jeez, I dunno," said the other guy. "I don't know of any place like that."

"Oh, man, I really need to crash," I sighed. "Is there a hippie part of town, you know, some kind of a street scene where there are a lot of freaks?"

"Sheeyit no," laughed the first guy. "You must be really lost. This is Fort Worth."

"I knew I shoulda toined left at Albukoiky," I groaned in my best Bugs Bunny voice.

They laughed, even the girl. She stepped out from behind the second guy, as if deciding I wasn't quite as scary as I looked.

"The only place we know where people go a lot is the Cellar. Maybe you could try there."

"The Cellar? What kind of a place is it?"

"Well, it's kind of a night club, I guess," she said. "They have drinks and music and you can dance if you want."

"And they have go-go girls," put in one of the guys.

"That sounds okay," I said. "And hippies go there?"

They all laughed. "Well, we may be the only hippies in Tarrant County, but there could be more. And if they were going out to party, they'd go to the Cellar. Every other bar is a cowboy shit-kicker bar."

"Okay," I said. "Where is it?"

"Just a few blocks from here," replied the girl. "That's where we're going. Come on."

I followed them through the urban streets of Fort Worth. It was getting dark already and neon lights were coming on up and down the streets. I regaled them with a hair-raising tale or two of my adventures getting there. Then we stopped at the top of a flight of stairs going down into one of those fenced-in stairwells. A hand-painted sign above the door designated it as The Cellar. The E's were funny, with just three horizontal strokes and no vertical. A bass guitar thumped from within. We filed down, paid a dollar cover charge, and pushed through a heavy velvet curtain.

It was dim and smoky inside, with lights flashing around the bar and one of those rotating light balls throwing colored beams through the smoke. Recorded rock and roll gushed out of the speakers mounted on every wall. There was a small stage in the middle with a round section extending at each end. There were three girls in bikinis doing the swim and the monkey and other nondescript dances on the stages. It was a big room, with maybe a hundred tables, but it seemed close with the low ceiling and all the walls and ceiling painted flat black. Above the stage was another The Cellar sign with funny E's.

We got a table, ordered drinks, and watched the girls dance. They were fairly attractive and easy to look at. They danced fairly dirty, like a strip joint, but they never took anything off. This was Fort Worth, after all. A few people were dancing on the dance floor in front of the stage. The girl we had come with danced with each of the other guys, and then I asked her to dance. I went into my usual spastic dance, spinning wildly around the floor with my hair flying out in a big circle around my head. I always dance barefoot, and my filthy feet were kicking up dust on the wood floor. She seemed mildly taken aback by my weird dancing style, but then everyone always was. She didn't seem inclined to repeat the experience, so I just sat and drank and watched the crowd, hoping to spot someone who might know a place I could crash.

The crowd was young and seemed moderately hip, but in a clean-cut provincial sort of way. They had paisley shirts and bellbottoms, sandals, and love beads, but there weren't many with long hair or truly extravagant dress. They seemed like young city people with jobs who thought the hippie scene was cool. After work they put on their hippie beads and totally unnecessary headbands and came down here to dance like they imagined they did it in Haight-Ashbury. Still, it felt much more comfortable than any other place I had been for quite a while, and I was enjoying myself. I was also trying not to think about how totally blank I was on how I might make contact with Elissa, if she'd even come to Fort Worth.

The go-go girls were constantly changing, and I realized they were also the cocktail waitresses. I started noticing one in particular, a tall statuesque blonde with a wonderful body and a nice smile. She was by far the best dancer, and there was always a crowd of guys hooting and hollering by the stage when she danced. I held myself above such shenanigans, but I had to admit she was a real fox. Most of the other girls looked like suburban Texas farm girls a little surprised to find themselves doing what they were. Most were indifferent dancers, swaying mechanically to the music in what they thought was seductive moves. But the blonde was different. She was really interpreting the music with her body, changing her moves with the changes in the music. She had a classically beautiful face, with high cheekbones and full sensual lips. Her eyes were a deep green and seemed a bit amused at all the hollering yokels. Watching her was getting me really turned on, and I was having fantasies about asking her for a place to stay. Once or twice I was sure she was looking at me with interest. Then her stint was done and she climbed down and picked up her drinks tray and started making the rounds. She came straight over to our table and I looked up at her in some surprise, wondering what opening line I should try. She looked at me quizzically. The kids with me seemed as surprised as I was to have this beautiful babe approach me.

"Is your name Brian?" she asked.

I was astonished. Here I was in a city I'd never been in before, in a bar I didn't know existed half an hour ago, and this beautiful chick seemed to know me. The theme of *Twilight Zone* came to mind.

"By a strange chance it actually is," I managed to reply.
One of the guys swallowed an ice cube in surprise.

Her face lit up with a huge smile. "Oh, wow," she laughed triumphantly. "I knew it. There can't be that many people with hair like that in this cow town. Hi, I'm Sammy."

"Hi, Sammy. How the hell do you know me?" I stammered.

"Because Elissa told me to keep an eye out for you," she said.

"Elissa?" I said, completely flabbergasted. "Is she here?"

"She's staying with me at my apartment."

"Really?" I gasped in disbelief. "But that's great. Hey, can I stay there, too?" Already I was having fantasies of a threesome with Sammy and Elissa.

Her smile faded. "Oh, well, I don't know about that, man, with you being so hot and all."

"Hot? Did Elissa tell you that?" I asked, pleased. "Well, she should know."

"No, not hot like that," she giggled. "I mean the cops are looking for you. You've been busted."

"Well, yeah. But I did my time, man. I just got out of the slammer." The kids at the table looked on in amazement at this strange conversation.

"No, I know about that. This is a new bust. You've been popped in Fort Worth, too."

Chapter Thirteen
Catching Up

"That can't be, man," I smiled. "I just got here an hour ago."

"Yeah, but your shit got here first, and the cops have it now and they're looking for you."

"Oh, man," I groaned. "Usually I can at least get to a place before I get busted there."

"It'll work out," she said cheerfully. "I gotta work now. I get off at eleven. Then I'll take you to meet Elissa."

"Okay, and thanks. Thanks a lot." She moved off and I again admired her figure. Guess that threesome probably wasn't going to work out, I mused sadly. I couldn't figure out about the bust. My stash was in a cookie tin in my duffel bag. The last I'd seen it, it was in the back of Sean's ambulance. But if the car had been busted, Elissa would be in the clink too. I resolved to worry about it later. I settled back to get drunk and enjoy the music. The kids I came with decided to leave early. No doubt they felt they'd fallen into bad company. Maybe they thought the place was going to get raided and they'd be caught in the crossfire.

It was a long time till she got off, but I didn't mind the wait. Sammy danced several more times. As the night got later and people got higher, the music got louder, the dancing got wilder, and the go-go girls cranked it up. They started to tease the crowd, like they were really going to strip. They'd pull their bra straps down and toy with the waistbands of their panties, but they never showed anything. One unfastened her top and danced for a while holding it up with her hands. The guys went wild, shouting for her to take it off, but stripping was illegal in Fort Worth and the club could have lost its license, so she was careful not to reveal anything. Still, the place became steamy with eroticism. Sammy was the best at it. She could drive the crowd wild with her dirty dancing. As soon as she climbed up on the stage the crowd would start cheering for her to do something. She seemed to enjoy the attention and played to it but never did more than tease and promise. I was in no hurry to leave.

When the place closed at two I was quite drunk and aroused from hours of dancing and watching Sammy. She changed and came out and collected me. I enjoyed the looks I got as we walked out together. In street clothes, Sammy was still attractive but not as spectacular and exotic as she had appeared on stage. I would still have jumped her in a minute, of course, but she gave me no encouragement. We walked out to her battered old VW bug and she drove me through the streets of Fort Worth, now mostly dark and empty.

"So about this bust," I said. "What happened?"

"Well, those people you were traveling with, Sean and Chris? They got busted. The car was searched and the cops found the dope in the guitar case. I guess your name was on it."

"Wait a minute. This doesn't make any sense. My stash wasn't in the case. And I am not quite stupid enough to put my name on my stash box: 'This illegal substance belongs to Brian. If lost or strayed, please call....' Not too cool."

"Well, I don't know exactly what happened. I guess Sean and Chris told the cops it was yours. I know the pigs are looking for you. It was in the newspaper even."

"Where are Sean and Chris?"

"They're in jail."

"Why didn't they take Elissa, too?"

"She wasn't with them at the time. They were being really shitty to her, so she came to stay with me."

"But she left my stuff in the car?"

"No, she took most of it to my place. But they still had your guitar. Sean wouldn't let her have it."

"Oh, man. What a towering heap of crap." I slumped down in the seat with disgust. I hated to think of all my beautiful stash in the hands of the cops. I tried to remember all the stuff I had in it. It was my best variety pack, hash and grass and speed and acid and lots of rare and exotic goodies from around the world, all carefully packaged in brightly colored little plastic boxes, and tastefully arranged to show off my wares to prospective buyers — and to impress girls. Gone, all gone. Not to mention my poor electric bass. By now I was so used to losing stuff, having it ripped off, or getting it confiscated by the authorities, that I was learning the Buddhist principle of nonattachment. Oh, well, less stuff to have to carry around and worry about.

"So how'd you meet Elissa?" I asked after a few minutes of grieving.

"She came into The Cellar one night looking for the scene, same as you. She asked me what the work was like. I guess she was getting pretty desperate for some cash. We got to talking. The poor kid didn't know where to go. So I let her crash with me. I like her a lot."

"Yeah, Elissa's great. Man, I was only in jail like a week. I thought she could just ride around with Sean and Chris for a while and then I'd find her again. They were jerks, but I didn't think they'd try to frame me."

We turned up a side street and she parked the car.

"Stay here," Sammy told me. "The cops know where Elissa is staying and I wouldn't be surprised if they were watching her to try to catch you."

"Oh, yeah," I sighed. "They probably are."

"What should we do?" she asked. "Maybe I should call her instead of going in."

"No, the line may be tapped. Why don't you go in and tell her I'm here? Tell her to go out like she's going for a walk. I'll meet her."

"Okay," she said nervously. We scanned the few cars parked along the street, trying to see if there were guys sitting in any of them. They appeared to be empty.

"Here goes," she said. She got out and walked away. I slid down in the seat and watched her disappear around a corner. Here we go again, I thought, scanning the parked cars and doorways for lurking figures. Back into the cops and robbers game they force you into. What a load of crap the drug laws are. They turn a huge number of otherwise law-abiding citizens into criminals. Whole organizations of tax-paid government employees are sent out to hunt these people down and lock them away for long intervals. And who benefited from all this? Nobody. Dope is only dangerous because it's illegal, which makes it expensive and forces you to deal with criminals to get it. If drugs were legal, there'd be no "drug problem." Why couldn't people see it? Didn't they learn anything from the first Prohibition?

Hunched down in the car seat, peering anxiously at every window and passing car, I felt like a resistance fighter in occupied France, with Nazis and informers everywhere. Why should it be like that for me?

This is my country too. Why can't I pursue my happiness? What's worse, I pay these guys who are hunting me – or I would be if my income were reportable. I found myself humming the Stephen Stills song *For What it's Worth* — "Paranoia strikes deep, into your life it will creep." If they were watching Elissa they'd probably follow her to me. I imagined a couple of suits approaching the car, trying to nail me. What would I do? I scouted a couple of possible escape routes between some of the old houses. I decided I didn't want to be caught in the car. I got out and strolled slowly along the street, listening for footsteps behind me, watching the shadows.

Then I heard someone coming. I slipped into the shadows beside a front stoop and waited. A woman appeared at the corner where Sammy had disappeared. She looked cautiously around, and then started walking toward me. When she got close enough I could see that it was Elissa, looking small and scared. I suddenly felt sorry for her. Here she was, eighteen years old, a small-town girl from Illinois, off on her first big adventure. Now she was scared and alone in a strange town, going to meet a wanted criminal on a seedy back street. This wasn't her scene at all. When she reached my hiding place I whispered her name. She jumped at the sound and turned to peer into the darkness.

"It's me," I said, and she flew into my arms.

"Oh, Brian," she gasped against my lips. "I have been so scared. I didn't know what to do. After you and Mike got busted we drove up here, but Sean and Chris were really mean to me. They wouldn't even stop when I had to pee."

"Why were they being such shits?"

"I think the cops down there in Roma and Rio Grande City really scared the shit out of them and they were blaming you and Mike for getting them into trouble. And they were taking it out on me."

"Those assholes. How'd the bust go down?"

"When we got here they found some people to stay with, but I didn't like them. They were hard and scary and mean to me, too. And Sean and Chris were still treating me like dirt, so I didn't want to stay there with them. I heard about the Cellar and went down there to see if I could get a job. Then I met Sammy and she invited me to stay with her, so I got all our stuff out of Sean's ambulance — all except your bass. Sean had started playing it a little and he said he wanted to keep it with him. I didn't want to let him, but he wouldn't listen to me. I thought maybe they were planning to skip town with it and just rip you off.

"Anyway, Sean was trying to sell some dope for a little spending money. One of the guys at the place they were staying wanted to buy but didn't have any money. He said he had an old set of weights — you know, barbells and stuff — at his parents' house. Sean agreed to help the guy pick them up and pawn them to get the cash. So one night when the guy's parents weren't home, they all drove over to this guy's parents' house and started hauling all these weights out of his garage and loading them into the ambulance. Some of the neighbors saw all these strange-looking people hauling shit out of the house and thought it was a burglary. They called the cops, and they caught them."

"Didn't the kid explain it was his house?"

"Yeah, but the whole thing looked suspicious, I guess. So they searched the car and found the shit in your guitar case."

"I didn't have any in there."

"I know. After you and Mike got busted, Sean was blaming you for all our troubles. He was really freaked out, like raging. Then on the drive up here a cop car came up behind us with his lights on and Sean panicked. The cop went right on past, but Sean was really paranoid. He had Chris put their stash in your guitar case so they could say they didn't know about it."

"That's sweet of him."

"Yeah. So when they got stopped in Fort Worth, he said it all belonged to this hitchhiker they had picked up and they hadn't known anything about it. Sean even told them where you were."

"What? Oh, man, that is so cold."

"The cops called Rio Grande City to have the sheriff send you up here. You must have gotten out just in time."

"When was this?"

"Two, no, three nights ago."

"Jesus. That was the same day Mike went back to the jail to see if our money had arrived. They must have called that same day after he left. And we just hung around town waiting for our money. I can't believe Sean was trying to fuck me over like that. What did I ever do to him?"

"I know. He was really different after the bust in Roma. That vigilante thing just freaked him out completely."

I stared at her sadly. Then a happy thought came to me. "Hey, so it was really Sean's stash that got popped? Where's mine?"

"I still have it. I hid it after all this stuff came down."

"Oh, you wonderful thing," I gushed, giving her a kiss. "Oh, baby, you did really great. I'm so sorry you got into this mess. If I'd known all this would happen, I'd never have suggested that you stay with Sean and Chris. But there was no place for you to hang down there."

She burst into tears. "I didn't want to leave you there in jail, honey. I just didn't know what else to do. We didn't have any money for a room or bail, even. And with you and Mike gone, Sean and Chris were just complete shits. I hate them."

"Well, it seems like you did everything you could. I'm sure glad you didn't get busted too."

"I know. If I'd stayed with them one more night I would have been there too. I was so scared when I heard about it. I didn't know what to do. I would have tried to leave town, but I knew you were coming here and I didn't want you to walk into this mess without knowing anything about it. So I've stayed here and been afraid to go out. I did call the cops and asked what was happening with Sean and Chris. At first they didn't want to tell me anything, but finally one guy told me that Sean and Chris were still being charged. They didn't really believe their story about not knowing the dope was there. They didn't really care about the guitar, but they wouldn't give it to me. They'd only release it to you. They said that if I heard from you I should tell you to come in and give your side of the story. They said if you did, they'd give your guitar back."

"Oh, yeah," I said. "Like I'm going to walk into the cop shop and say, 'Yeah, I'm the guy who owns the guitar case. You know, the one full of dope. Can I have it back, please?' I don't think so."

"I don't know, honey. They might be telling the truth. They're busting Sean and Chris anyway. They didn't even try to charge me. I don't think they want to bust you. They just want to hear your side of the story."

"No way I'm going in there," I replied. "I can't think of anything I could say or do that would help Sean and Chris, and I don't have any strong urge to risk my neck for them. The cops can keep the damn guitar. Hey, maybe one of them will try it out. The guys down at the station can get a rock band together – The Psychedelic Pigs or something."

She smiled at that, the first smile I'd seen. I realized how scared she'd been, and still was. I had to get her out of this situation. But how? We were broke and didn't know anybody in the state. The only person we did know was Sammy. There was nowhere else to go.

"Elissa," I said. "I don't think there's anyone watching you. I checked out the street pretty carefully and didn't see anything. That doesn't mean they're not there, but I don't think we're big enough fish for them to put a tail on you. We need to talk to Sammy right away."

She hesitated, looking about at the dark buildings around us, then nodded.

"Then let's walk together, like a couple. If they're looking for one of us, they might pay less attention to us together." We started back toward the apartment, with her snuggled up against me and my arm around her shoulders, like the cover of *Highway 61 Revisited*. Man, she felt good to me. I was so happy to find her.

We went to Sammy's apartment and she let us in. It was a small unattractive place, but clean. She had put some psychedelic posters on the dingy walls in an attempt to liven it up. We got out my stash and passed a pipe or two as we caught up on the news. Sammy obviously knew all about Elissa's travails so far, but she asked a lot of questions about my jail experience in Rio Grande City.

The smoke made me realize how hungry I was. The girls were, too. Sammy fixed something to eat and we sat around the kitchen table and talked as we ate.

"Listen, Elissa," said Sammy. "You know I love you, girl, but you two cannot stay here. I can't afford trouble. Dancing just barely pays for this dump, and this is the bottom rung. I can't afford to lose my job."

"I know, Sammy," said Elissa. "We understand. You've been great to take me in and help me when I was completely at the end of my rope. I'll never forget that."

"Yeah," I said. "I don't want to get anybody in any more trouble, least of all to the one person who's been nice to Elissa. But where can we go? We don't know anybody here."

"Where do you usually go? Elissa says you've been on the road for months."

"Well, yeah. But for part of it we were on a bus, and for most of the rest we were in an ambulance. So we always had places to sleep on the road. And we went to towns that were known to have hippie communities: Denver, Boulder, and Taos. I figured I could just walk into Fort Worth and find a free place to crash. I'm stuck here."

"I'm trying to think who might help you," said Sammy. "There are a couple of houses around where some hippies live. But I only know one guy who lives in one."

"Do you know how to contact him?" I asked.

"Yeah, I have his number, I think."

"Would they take us in, do you think?"

"Well, it's not really a crash pad. Just a few people live there. But they might let you stay there."

"Yeah, it's worth a try," I said. Already I was thinking that a freak family in the middle of cowville might be very happy indeed to see a man with a tin can full of dope.

Sammy looked up the number in her notebook. "Yeah, here it is. Joe Lowry."

Chapter Fourteen
Hey Joe

"Do you mind calling him?" I asked her. "If you don't feel comfortable doing it, that's okay. We'll think of something. We're not your responsibility, you know."

"Yeah, I know. But I can't just turn you out on the sidewalk, can I?" She called the number.

"Joe? It's Sammy. Yeah, hi. Yes, it has. Too long. Listen, can I ask you a funny question? Yeah? Okay. Do you think Jim and Bev would let a couple of strangers stay with you guys at their place?"

She listened for a while in silence. Elissa and I strained to hear the tinny little voice at the other end.

"Well, they're not exactly runaways, no," Sammy said. "They're not kids. They're from out of town and they've gotten into a bit of a jam." She waited for his question. "Well, a legal jam. They're a little hot, but nice, really, both of them," she added quickly.

"Well, for drugs. Some people they know got busted a few nights ago and the police want to talk to them. No, not exactly. No. No. No, they didn't confiscate it. Yes. Well, maybe. Yeah, probably. You will? Great. Come on over to my place, then."

She hung up and looked at us with a broad grin. "He'll do it. He's going to ask Jim and Bev, they're the ones that own the place, it it's all right with them. But he's pretty sure it will be."

"Great!" I shouted, and Elissa's face relaxed immediately. It's astounding how stressful it is to not know where you're going to sleep. It's a hard feeling to get used to. When I'm just living on the street, every day I first figure out where I'm going to stay the next night. Sometimes it's a hassle. Sometimes it takes most of the day. But once it's settled, then I can enjoy the rest of the day. Food is easier to find and less stressful. I can always find something to eat. But sleeping under a bush or on a fire escape is a miserable way to spend the night. And you're completely vulnerable to anybody who stumbles on you.

We rapped for a while, and then there was a knock at the door. There was a momentary panic while we whisked the paraphernalia out of sight and got ourselves together, then Sammy went to the door.

"Who is it?" she asked.

"Joe," came the welcome reply, and she admitted a tall, chubby guy about nineteen or twenty. He looked like your average Midwestern farm boy. He had an open, friendly face and he looked us over curiously as we were introduced.

We sat and talked and told him our story. I brought out the pipe again and filled it with my best Afghani hashish. There's a time to pull out all the stops to make a favorable impression. The hash worked with its wonted efficiency and soon we were all giggling together like old friends. We asked him about the house where he lived.

"Oh, it's great," Joe said. "It's this normal-looking house in the suburbs where a young married couple just turned on and dropped out. They still work and stuff, but they let all these other freaks live in their house and they get high a lot. They're really cool."

"How many people live there?" Elissa asked.

"Well, there's Jim and Bev and their baby, and Martha, and Sue, and me, sometimes. I still live at home sometimes, but I go over there whenever I can. There's always something happening."

"And you think Jim and Bev would let us stay there a while?"

"Sure, I think so. Shit, man. You bring hash like this, they might let you sleep in their bed."

"Okay," I said. "Let's go see them. You got a car?"

"Yeah, are you ready?"

"It'll just take a few minutes," said Elissa. She went to get her stuff together. Sammy lugged out my ratty old army duffel bag. It was like seeing an old friend. And I could change clothes for the first time in about ten days. Elissa brought out her little blue suitcase. She and Sammy hugged and we both thanked her for all her help.

"Bye, guys," she said. "Good luck. Bye, Joe."

We went out and squeezed into Joe's VW bug. We rolled slowly through the empty streets of Fort Worth for what seemed like many miles, until the tall buildings were just a smudge of light on the horizon. Finally we turned onto McCart Street and rolled to a stop in front of a white frame house on a corner. It looked exactly like every other house in the neighborhood. It must have been two in the morning by then.

"This is it," said Joe. "Chez Carter, or That Damned Hippie House, depending on your point of view."

We hauled our stuff up onto the porch and Joe led us in without even knocking. We stepped into a little entryway. Through a doorway I could see a darkened living room. I expected June Cleaver to appear around a corner, crying, "Hippies! In my clean living room!"

Instead, there were four or five freaks, guys and chicks, lying around on the floor listening to music in near darkness. They ranged in appearance from only slightly bizarre to looking like narcs – a little too clean for real hippies. They looked up at us in some surprise.

One guy got up to greet us. He was very tall and thin, with that straight-backed, long-necked, exceptionally clean look I associate with Mormons. He had blond hair cut short, a short-sleeved white shirt, and an intelligent open face.

"Hey, Joe," he said.

"Hey, Jim. This is Brian and Elissa. They're from Back East. Guys, this is Jim Carter. He owns this place."

"Hi, Jim," I said. On the way over I had been working on a speech to try to talk him into letting us stay there. It was full of pathos and human tragedy, playing us up like lost waifs thrown upon the strange shores of Fort Worth. But I was taken aback by how straight these people looked. And Joe said Jim owned the house. I'd never met an actual homeowner before. What were the chances these people would let a couple of unknown drifters into their home?

"Hi," said Jim. "You guys need a place to crash?"

Elissa suddenly laughed, and I realized how nervous she had been. Poor kid, she'd never lived on the street before. She must have been so scared all this time.

"Oh, do we ever, man," I said. "It would be so great if we could just stay here a few days. We don't have any bread…"

Jim waved away my words. "Don't need it here, man," he said. "This house is a port of refuge. You can stay here as long as you like."

Chapter Fifteen
Port of Refuge

I was literally overwhelmed. I had been in plenty of crash pads —
usually ratty tenement apartments filled with smelly street people. I
usually never even knew who paid the rent, if anybody. But this was
completely different. These were people who really owned this house.
This was their furniture, TV, knickknacks on the shelves. It took real
conviction to open up their house like this to perfect strangers — and
some courage. They didn't know us at all. This was living the hippie
creed to the max.

"Wow, that is so hip," I said sincerely. "Thanks, brother."

He brought us into the living room to meet the others. A tall, slim,
pretty blonde woman got up.

"This is my wife Bev," said Jim. "Honey, this is Brian and Elissa.
They'd like to stay here awhile."

Bev looked as straight and clean-cut as Jim did. They looked a lot
like an older Ken and Barbie. She could've been any suburban
housewife. From my limited experience with married couples, I
immediately expected her to say, "What do you mean, they're staying
here?" I started a pre-emptive move.

"We'll just be here a few days," I said hurriedly. "We're on our
way to California." I resisted the impulse to add, "Ma'am."

Her face lit up with a big smile. "Oh, that's great! Come on in.
Sit down. Is that all your shit? Just dump it beside the door till we
figure out where everybody's going to crash."

I relaxed immediately. This place was not what it appeared. I
realized I had a prejudice to overcome. Just because they looked
straight and talked with a soft Texan accent, these people were very
cool. This may be the boondocks, but they weren't just reading about
the hippies in Life Magazine and putting on some beads. They
believed in the lifestyle, and were living it.

We met their friends. Martha was a big tall heavy woman who looked a bit like Mama Cass. She had a big booming laugh and talked dirty for a girl. Then there were two guys sitting together. Rick looked like a Texas good ole boy. He was thin and rangy and wore a cowboy shirt with the button pockets and all. He had the lazy relaxed moves and lopsided grin of a cowboy, too. The other guy Ron I couldn't figure out. He was very small and dark, with a round head, horn-rimmed glasses, and one of those short chins and wide lip-less mouths like old toothless codgers get, so his mouth tended to disappear under his large nose. He was definitely an odd-looking guy. It was hard to guess his age, but he didn't appear over twenty-five or so. He had odd, rather girlish mannerisms, too, and a high-pitched giggle that always made me laugh. His name was Ron, but was usually called Puss for no reason I could imagine.

They were all very nice and welcomed us to join them. They had obviously known each other a long time and had lots of little in-jokes and digs at each other. They seemed to all really like each other. They had a tiny baggie of dope and we passed around a bong.

Watching them, I recognized again how lonely it is on the road, always surrounded by strangers. Because I was never with people I knew, I always felt that I was on stage or something, like I had to act a part. I had eventually found a role I was comfortable with — I was the ultra-cool traveling dope dealer, full of wild stories of the street. People liked that stuff, enjoyed hearing my rap. I was welcome in a crash pad. But I was never in one place long enough to make friends. People drifted past, and I'd usually never know their last names. Watching these people laugh and talk, I envied them their closeness.

Elissa was generally quiet, but seemed to be enjoying herself. She sat next to me, holding my hand, and I think we were both just happy to be together and feel safe again. I'd been on the road a long time already and knew how to do it, but there's always an element of fear out there. You're totally vulnerable on the road, and you never know when you're going to run across some psycho. Lots of people hated hippies on sight, especially here in the south. I'd be a perfect victim for some redneck sadist. There wasn't a person in the world that knew where I was. I didn't run scared all the time, of course, but the thought occurred. It must have been really scary for poor Elissa. She was just a kid, fresh out of her freshman year in college, and all this was completely new to her. Anyway, we stayed close and enjoyed the conversation.

They asked us how we came to be there, and we gave them a brief outline of The Story So Far. They seemed impressed by our encounter with the vigilantes and the recent bust. They asked us a lot about Sean and Chris and the trip in the ambulance. We regaled them with stories of the Elysian fields of peyote down in South Texas, and how unreachable they were. I waxed poetic about the joys of a peyote high, which none of them had ever done.

Then Jim announced that we had to put the bong away because he was about out of dope. There were groans all around. I glanced at Elissa with a grin.

"Anybody like to do some hash, then?" I asked innocently. The response was immediate and enthusiastic. One or two had tried hash before, but the others knew nothing about it. I went to my duffel bag and pulled out my old stash, an old Christmas cookie tin, and pulled off the lid. Everyone gathered around to peer inside. There were dozens of brightly colored little plastic boxes inside, each containing a different drug. There were two pipes, a steamroller, and a small folding bong. The interstices were packed with small packages of cloth or aluminum foil, roach clips, and four different types of rolling papers. There was a collective gasp.

I extracted one bright red box and shook its contents into my palm — a lump of shiny black hashish as big as my thumb. "This is Afghani kif," I said, "scraped from the bodies of naked virgins after they run through the flowering fields." More exclamations of wonder. I was in my element. "Kif is made from marijuana pollen, but much stronger, and the high is quite a bit different," I explained, as I extracted my stiletto knife from my boot and shaved off a sizable chunk. "It's a brighter, sharper-edged high, sometimes with almost psychedelic visuals." I dropped the chunk into my carved wooden pipe.

"Afghani can be a little harsh," I continued, "so I like to mellow it with some Lebanese brown." I took out a smaller yellow box and shook out an irregular lump of what looked like light brown mud. I broke off a piece and crumbled it into the bowl, tamping it firmly with my chrome pipe tamper. I looked around at the others. They were staring silently, as if watching a religious ceremony. "Anybody like to try some?" I asked. That broke the spell, and we all gathered into a small circle for passing.

I lit off the pipe, took an immense hit, and then passed it to Elissa. She grinned at me and did a good toke, then passed it on to Jim. That killed conversation for a while, as we were all flying in seconds. By the time the pipe completed its first round, no one was sitting up any longer. It was some time before anyone spoke, and then it was Puss exclaiming in a reverent whisper, "Holy fucking shit."

I pushed myself back up into a sitting posture and pulled my stash toward me. "Yeah, not bad. How about some Vietnamese black, this time, just to take the edge off?" Elissa smiled at me from the corner. We were in.

Sometime around four or five in the morning, Jim and Bev retired to their bedroom, and soon after, the others left. Elissa and I cuddled into my ratty old single sleeping bag and did what we'd been wanting to all night. It was great to be together again. For the first time in months, we felt safe.

Chapter Sixteen
The McCart Street Commune

At seven I woke up enough to find Jim and Bev moving about. Jim was in a suit and tie and Bev looked great in a pastel business suit. I realized with astonishment that they were off to work. Not only did they maintain this incredible hippie crash pad all night, but they also held down respectable jobs by day. My respect for them went up several more notches.

We woke up much later and had another nice slow one. Then we puttered about the house, cleaning up the mess and doing a pile of dirty dishes. It seemed the least we could do for the kindness they'd shown us. In the middle of the afternoon, Joe and Martha dropped by and we started up the bong again. At six, Jim and Bev got home, changed into civilian clothes, and the party started again in earnest. Three or four friends dropped in during the evening, and the party went late again.

After a week, I decided to see if I could find out what was going on with the bust. Using a pay phone, I called the Dallas cops and inquired about Sean and Chris and my guitar. They said that, under questioning, Sean had blown it by admitting that he knew the dope was in the guitar case, so they were definitely busted. After that, it didn't matter where they got the stuff. So they weren't looking for me. There didn't seem to be anything we could do to help Sean and Chris. I asked the cops if my guitar case was evidence, and they said no, just the dope bag they'd taken out of it. I asked if I could have it back and they said sure, just come by and pick it up. They told me there was no warrant out for me. I wasn't quite that trusting, but Joe volunteered to go down and get it, which he did with no hassle. So I even got my bass back.

By this time we'd become quite close with Jim and Bev. They were both great kind people, and very bright. We often had deep philosophical and political talks late into the night. Jim and I in particular seemed to think alike in many ways. I told Jim and Bev that I'd finished my business in Fort Worth and we were ready to move on, but they both asked us to stay on. We put the word out that we were looking for a ride to California, but we were in no particular hurry. Since we were broke anyway and didn't know how we were going to continue to California, it was great to have a good place to stay. There was no discussion of how long we could stay.

So life continued in the incredible McCart Street crash pad. There was continuous partying, and on weekends there were often twenty or thirty people lying around getting high. Tarrant County Junior College (TCJC to the cognoscenti) was nearby, and a number of kids from the school spent their weekends at the Carter place. There was a constant coming and going of people, and all were fun to be around.

Elissa and I became minor celebrities, mainly because we'd been outside of Texas. The others seemed to think we were pretty cool. I sometimes regaled the party with tales of dope deals on the Lower East Side or my adventures the summer before in fabled Haight-Ashbury. It came to seem sometimes that I was holding court, with a dozen or so starry-eyed hippies gathered around listening to my stories. I was becoming something of a local legend, and was enjoying the notoriety.

We got to know the regulars better; the ones we'd met that first night. Martha was very funny and loved to tell dirty jokes. Rick and Ron, it turned out, were gay lovers. They were completely open and blatant about it, which was shocking even to me (the gay movement had not begun to come out at that time), and absolutely mind-blowing in central Texas. We learned that Ron's nickname Puss was short for Pussyface, for obvious reasons, and his classic Karmann Ghia was known to all as the Pussymobile. They seemed to be happy and in love and completely unashamed. They changed my attitude towards gays forever.

There was also a lot of straight sex going on. I was pretty sure some of the women in the family might be available, maybe even Bev, but I thought it best to ignore that. Some of the young Texas college girls that came by on weekends were really hot, though. There were a number of girls that I thought might be interested in me. Much as I liked Elissa, the first dark thoughts began to arise that she was keeping me from sampling a lot of other girls.

Chapter Seventeen
A Day in the Park

It was getting to be late March, and springtime had finally arrived in Texas. The last day of March was to be my twenty-first birthday, the day I was finally to become an adult. For a few days there had been talk of the whole family going out somewhere for a picnic to enjoy the spring weather. That day was a Sunday, and it dawned warm and bright and perfect. It was the first really warm day after a long cold winter. We decided to go to the city botanical gardens, have a picnic, and celebrate my coming of age. We packed food, Frisbees, bubble wands, streamers, and blankets into several cars, smoked a huge amount of dope to tide us over for a few hours, and headed for the park.

This was quite an outing for the family. Texas was not accepting of hippies and there was a lot of fear and hostility. We were all accustomed to getting hostile stares and shouted comments when we went out. Because of that, most of the family members didn't look all that different from straight folks, but it didn't take much hair to make a guy stand out in Texas in those days. Rick and Ron would have stood out anywhere; and my headband and hair down past my shoulder blades was a positive affront to Texan patriotism and manhood. So we had kept our lifestyle pretty much out of sight all winter. But today was just too pretty to stay indoors.

We knew we weren't the only hippies in Fort Worth. Occasionally one of us would spot another longhair around town and we'd flash the peace sign to each other. We figured there must be another family hiding out somewhere. But we were totally unprepared for the scene in the park.

I guess everybody else had the same idea, because the park was jammed with people. And not just rednecks — there were literally hundreds of hippies out enjoying the sunshine, and if I was any judge of a high, we weren't the only ones stoned out. In a more enlightened city the air would be blue with smoke, but not in Fort Worth in 1968.

Like us, everyone had lifted off at home, and then come out to the park. There were people playing guitars, people drumming, pretty girls dancing, people playing Frisbee, and many just lying in the grass enjoying the day. It was a beautiful park, with pools and fountains and little shady dells surrounded by flowers. A few people were wading in the pools, laughing and splashing each other. It was a

Figure 1. Hippies arriving at the Botanical Gardens

beautiful sight. I liked to think the entire hippie population of Fort Worth had turned out to help me celebrate my birthday. We were astonished to see so many hippies, and everybody else seemed to be just as surprised.

Figure 2. More locals. Alyse Dar in center.

The authorities certainly were surprised. I don't know how it started. Perhaps some outraged citizens called the cops; maybe the park police thought we were a demonstration or a riot and called for reinforcements; maybe the mayor looked out his window and thought they were being invaded. But Fort Worth was clearly not ready for hippies in their park.

Suddenly there were cops everywhere. Eight or ten cars pulled up all around the park and guys in suits and uniforms came running across the grass toward us. A black-and-white came roaring right up the sidewalk, lights flashing and siren ripping the quiet summer air. Six cops jumped out and leaped on the nearest people, wrestling them to the ground and screaming in their faces. Girls started screaming. I could hear shouts and curses. People started running in every direction.

I was sitting in the shade under a big tree with a half dozen of the family. I had been in enough busts and police actions to know it was time to get the hell out of there. "Everybody split up!" I hissed. "Get away from each other. Walk away — don't run, that can draw a shot in the back." Elissa looked at me in alarm. "Go on, babe. Try to get back to the house." I immediately got up and started walking quickly away from the center of the fracas. I repeated my mantra: don't look around; don't draw attention; make no threatening gestures. I reached the edge of the park and blended into the crowd watching the cops slamming people around. I gently sidled toward the back of the crowd, thinking to slink quietly away.

I hadn't gone fifty feet when four cops ran straight up to me, pushing the crowd roughly aside.

"There's one of them!" shouted one red-faced, beefy cop. "Get 'im!" yelled another.

I didn't know why I was so popular, but I knew better than to resist. I stopped and turned to face them, my hands open and out. Two of them grabbed my hands and twisted them behind

Figure 3. Brian at the Gardens, March 31, 1968

119

my back, doubling me over onto my knees and pressing my face into the ground. "Gotcha, you sumbitch," one of them shouted in my ear.

One cop held me like that while another frisked me. He pulled out the long narrow folding knife I always carried. "Whew, look at this, Leroy," he said, opening it and waving it around. "This boy's carrying a concealed weapon. Hang onto him." Then he and the other cops ran off to beat up somebody else.

My hair had come loose and was covering my face, but I could see that I was in the middle of a crowd of people, all staring at me in fear and wonder. "What's going on?" somebody said. "Why are they doing that?" asked somebody else. "Who is that guy?" "What did that man do, Mommy?"

I just held still and waited to see what would happen next. The cop holding me had a gun and a big heavy wooden nightstick and I was in no hurry to get acquainted with either one. I didn't know what they could charge me with. I didn't think the knife was illegal. We'd all been very careful to not be holding any dope, knowing we were going out in public. I hoped that I'd be let go with a warning to get the hell out of Texas. Right then, I was more than willing to do just that.

It didn't take long for all the running and shouting to settle down. Then the cop holding me pulled me to my feet and pushed me along the street that ran beside the park. I could see five or six others being led the same direction. Considering there must have been a hundred or more of us in the park, it didn't seem like a big haul of prisoners. As they brought us together, though, and we looked at each other, I realized what the scene was. I didn't know any of them, but we were all guys, and we all had long hair. They didn't want to catch everybody, just the "ringleaders." And obviously, the guys with the longest hair must be the leaders. Real native-born Texas boys would never wear their hair like a girl's, so we must be Yankee commie agitators, sent down here to turn their boys into pinkos and pollute their womenfolk. They loaded us into a paddy wagon and took us off to jail.

Chapter Eighteen
Birthday Bust

This was already my third bust, so I was beginning to know the routine. We were booked, printed, and photographed, then dumped into a holding tank with a bunch of winos and petty crooks. After a while, they took us out one by one for questioning. I was shown into an examining room, where a guy in a suit was waiting for me behind a table. He waved me to a metal chair across from him.

He asked me my name, which I told him. I had no intention of leading him to the family, so I said I had no address. I said I was a college kid traveling across Texas and just passing through Fort Worth. I was tired and went to the park to rest. I had no idea what all those other people were doing there; I didn't know anyone there; I didn't know why I was in jail. "It's not illegal to go to a park in this town, is it?"

"It may be for you, kid," he said.

"What are the charges?"

"Carrying a concealed weapon, for one. That switchblade you got."

"Come on. It's a penknife. It's legal if it's less than five-and-a-half inches, and mine's five inches. It was a gift from my Dad." This wasn't true, of course, but I wanted him to know I had a dad. People with no connections can wind up missing.

"We got you for loitering, too."

"Loitering? Come on, it's a public park. You're supposed to loiter there. That's why they build parks."

"And vagrancy."

"Vagrancy? What the hell is that? I'm a tourist. What makes me a vagrant?"

"You had less than ten dollars on you when we picked you up."

"So what?"

"Under the civil code, anybody with less than ten dollars is by definition a vagrant. That's thirty days."

"Bullshit. I just lost my wallet."

"Tell it to the judge, kid." He called for the guard and I was led back to the tank.

Now I was depressed. Here it was, my twenty-first birthday, and I was back in jail. I figured the weapons charge and the loitering were bullshit, but I didn't know about the vagrancy. If it really was illegal to have less than ten dollars, I was guilty. And I couldn't think of a damn thing to do about it. I sure couldn't afford a lawyer, and nobody even knew where I was. I assumed I would eventually be allowed a phone call, and I was steeling myself to have to call my parents. They'd think I was calling because it was my birthday and would be pleased to take the call. Then I'd have to tell them I was in jail again. And how long would I have to stay here? There'd be a wait for an indictment, then a wait for a trial, and then thirty days in jail. What a crock. I sank into a deep depression. How could a day that started so beautifully end up so shitty?

Late that afternoon, a guard came to the door and called my name. I got up and went to the door.

"Yeah?"

"Grab your shit, kid. You're outa here."

"What? How come?"

"You met bail."

"Can't be. Nobody even knows I'm here."

"So you staying in?"

"No, no, I'm with you, man." He unlocked the door and led me down a long green corridor. I kept trying to think what all this meant. All I could think was that there had been a screw-up and they'd gotten the names wrong. The only person who knew me was Elissa, and she didn't have a dime. At the end of the corridor I waited in a room with a bunch of other guys while a clerk handed out people's belongings. When my turn came I went up to the counter and was handed a plastic baggie with my headband, belt, and knife. I took it and was shown to a door. When I went through it, there was Jim Carter waiting for me.

"Jim! What the hell are you doing here?"

He grinned at me. "I bailed you out, man."

I couldn't believe it. Here I was, some drifter he didn't know at all. He'd let me stay in his place, fed me, and now he was risking his neck and a bunch of money to bail me out of jail?

"You did?" I stammered. "What the hell for?"

"Couldn't let you spend your birthday in jail, could I?"

He told me the bail was two hundred dollars. I was overwhelmed. I thanked him over and over, totally knocked out by his kindness and trust. I swore I wouldn't let him lose his bail money.

"I know you wouldn't," he said. "Come on, let's get out of this dump."

We went out to his car and headed for home. He told me that nobody else in the family had had any trouble. They did what I said and scattered, then met back at the car. I asked if they saw me getting popped.

"Sure, man. Everybody did. Didn't you see the TV camera?"

"No, I kind of had my head on the cement. What camera?"

"A local station had a crew there, right next to where they grabbed you. They had the camera right on you when they were busting you. It was cool."

"Yeah, it was great. My fifteen seconds of fame."

"No, really, it was pretty neat." Jim was excited; he thought it all very exciting. "Everybody was all outraged, even the straights. They were all asking what you had done."

"I was wondering that myself," I said. "They charged me with a concealed weapon, vagrancy, and loitering."

"That's all bullshit," said Jim. "They'll never make any of that stick."

"Man, you're driving fast, Jim," I observed. "Take it easy, let's not get busted again."

"Hey, I want to get home before the evening news. You'll be on it for sure, and it's just a few minutes before six."

I settled back. Now that I was out, I was feeling a lot better. And Jim's incredibly generous gesture really touched me. I wasn't alone after all; I had friends. And the idea of being on the news started to appeal. I wanted to see what the bust looked like.

We screeched into Jim's driveway and ran into the house. It was full of people — all the usual suspects, plus ten or fifteen of the weekend hangers-on. They were all gathered around the television. Bev was passing around popcorn. They all jumped up when we came in. Elissa squealed and threw her arms around me. There was a huge commotion as people congratulated me and slapped me on the back and shook my hand. It made me feel great. From feeling very scared and alone, I was back in the bosom of family. Suddenly Joe was shouting for everybody to shut up. "Shut up, god damn it, the news is coming on!"

We all quieted down and sat down to watch. There was a shot of the White House, flags snapping in the cold Washington wind. The news guy came on, hair and tan perfect. He looked very serious.

"Today is Sunday, March 31, 1968. Today, President Lyndon Johnson announced that he will not seek re-election. He will retire at the end of his term in January."

"Hot damn!" somebody yelled. "He's quitting, can you believe that?" Everybody was talking at once. We were all thrilled and excited. For years now Johnson had represented the enemy, the main driving force keeping us in the war in Vietnam. He'd escalated the war, started carpet-bombing of Hanoi. He'd directed the police to stop the unrest in the streets, instigating countless police beatings of blacks and hippies. He was the leader of the forces opposed to the hippie movement. And he was giving up. It was completely unexpected news, and very welcome. We were winning. The people were finally winning.

There was the usual war story, footage of guys in camouflage creeping through the jungle, helicopters firing rockets, exploding balls of napalm, wounded guys being carried to helicopters. The usual unbelievable body counts: twenty-five Americans killed, five hundred Viet Cong.

There was so much talk going on about Johnson that we almost missed my story. But then it went to local news. There was a shot of people running in the park. "There was a demonstration today in the Fort Worth Botanical Gardens. Young hooligans disrupted a quiet Sunday in the park, frightening local families." There were shots of a couple dancing in a fountain, obviously terrorizing citizens. "Police made a number of arrests." Then there was a shot of a young guy with no shirt and long greasy brown hair being wrestled to the ground by three cops. The crowd around me yelped in delight, and I realized it was me. The camera moved in close as they frisked me. When they opened the knife and held it up, the camera made a long slow pan all the way down the blade and back up, as if it were a saber or something. It was so silly we all broke up laughing. Then there was a shot of me being hustled into the back of a paddy wagon with the other unlucky ones, and the wagon pulling away, peace signs waving out the windows, leaving the city once more safe for law-abiding citizens.

When it was over, there was cheering and whistling. They seemed to think I had done a fine job of portraying the poor innocent hippie being savagely abused by the pigs. It certainly added to my fame, and I was starting to enjoy it. My birthday turned out to be a pretty good day after all.

Chapter Nineteen
Civil Liberties

One thing the bust changed was that we were stuck in Fort Worth while the wheels of justice slowly turned. We had several discussions about what I should do. Then Bev suggested I contact the American Civil Liberties Union. I didn't think they'd be interested in my case; they mostly defended Communists and Nazis and other downtrodden masses, big high-profile cases involving major ethical issues. Mine was just an ordinary bust. But Joe and Jim agreed it was worth a try, and the next day Jim called them. It turned out they were very interested. They asked me to come down to their offices to talk it over.

When I met the ACLU attorney, he was very nice. He agreed the weapons charge and the loitering charge were nonsense and would be dropped. But he was very interested in the vagrancy charge. It turned out that the ACLU had been looking for a good clean vagrancy case for a long time. The vagrancy statutes are nothing more or less than a law against being poor, which is clearly unconstitutional. But a hell of a lot of people were doing time just for being short of cash. Lots of jurisdictions had such laws, mostly just as a means of locking up people they didn't like and getting them off their streets. Most often the charges were never pursued. The cops would tell the guy there're letting him go this time, but he'd better beat it out of town or they'd run him in for good. Most people would leave town, so relatively few vagrancy cases ever actually came to court. Those that did were often combined with other charges, like public drunkenness, urinating in public, shoplifting, or some other misdemeanor.

What the ACLU wanted was a straightforward case, where the accused was clearly guilty of nothing more than being broke. I seemed to fit the bill. The case already had some visibility from the news story. The TV coverage clearly showed that I wasn't doing anything and wasn't resisting arrest. The lawyer asked me to describe everything that happened that day at the park.

When he'd heard my account of the arrest, the ACLU attorney was positively salivating. "Mr. Crawford," he said. "The ACLU will be happy to take your case, pro bono — that means at no charge to you." Ecstatic and relieved, I started to thank him profusely, but he interrupted me. "But you should understand one thing. We are hoping you will be convicted."

My grin collapsed. "What? You want me to lose the case?"

"Yes. You see, if they drop the charges, the case is over and the statute will remain in place for use against others. But if you're convicted, we would appeal the case. What we're hoping is that you will lose again and again and the case will move up through the courts and end up in the Supreme Court. That's where we think we can win, where the statute comes up against the constitution. We've already had people working on a defense for the Supreme Court. If we win there, vagrancy statutes will be declared unconstitutional, and every single one will have to be stricken from the books, all over the country. Never again will it be possible to jail people just for being poor."

"Wow," I murmured. "It would be like the Miranda Decision."

"Exactly. You would be instrumental in getting vagrancy laws thrown out forever."

"That would be great."

"You must understand that it could take a long time; perhaps years. And until then you would be convicted. You might have to spend more time in jail, though the ACLU would provide bail, of course."

"Oh. Yeah, I see what you mean. So I'd have to hang around and be ready to go to court all those times."

"Yes. It would require a real commitment on your part. The prosecutors would no doubt offer you deals, to drop the charges, clear your record. We would want you to reject the deals and take the sentence so we could appeal again. Are you willing to do that?"

I thought about it a long time. That was a lot more time and commitment than I'd given anything in years. But then I thought of the cops breaking up that beautiful day in the park, scaring people and roughing up kids for no reason at all. It was wrong, and it should be stopped. Maybe I was just the guy to do it. What the hell, it wasn't like my schedule was full or anything. I looked at the lawyer. "Sure, yeah, I'll do it."

He looked really pleased. "Wonderful. I'll have some papers for you to sign, authorizing the ACLU to represent you. Your indictment has been set for May 15th."

"Jesus, that's a long time away."

"Yes. As I said, it's a slow process. They're no doubt hoping you plead guilty, pay the fine, and get out of town."

"Not me," I said. "I'm going for the Crawford Decision."

When I got back to the house, I explained the whole situation to the family. They were as excited as I was. "Oh, man," said Joe. "Wouldn't you love to see the cops have to eat their words and let everybody go they have locked up for vagrancy?"

"That would be so cool," said Jim.

"But that means we have to stay here a lot longer, right?" asked Elissa. She was still hot to get out to California. But I was having fun in Fort Worth and was no longer in a hurry to go.

Chapter Twenty
The Scene of the Crime

Life continued in the same vein for the next month, with smoking and partying day and night and full-on heavy duty partying every weekend. Jim and I were often the last ones still awake in the wee hours, talking about everything from politics to religion to metaphysics to astronomy. Jim liked to hear my stories of the exotic drugs I'd encountered. About the only thing they ever got in Fort Worth was a fairly weak local grass known as Waxahachie Green. My stash of exotics was running low and I was saving it for special occasions. We'd done some speed and acid, but I was nearly out of that, too.

Jim kept asking me about the peyote fields down in Roma where I'd been busted. We talked again and again about what a shame it was that the fields were right along the Rio Grande, right under the noses of the Border Patrol.

"We did a couple of things wrong," I said. "First, we were very conspicuous. A whole bunch of hippies in a red Cadillac ambulance aren't going to go unnoticed in South Texas. Second, we went into Roma to have dinner the night before the raid. That was really dumb. Third, we spent the night in the car out near the fields, increasing the chances of being spotted. And fourth, we were too greedy. Mike and I had two sleeping bags stuffed full of buttons in the first hour. I don't know how many buttons that is, but a couple thousand for sure. At five bucks a button, that's ten grand. If we had just quit then and laid low under a bush until after dark, we'd never have been spotted."

"So it seems to me," said Jim thoughtfully, "that a couple of enterprising guys could drive down there unobtrusively, arrive in the middle of the night, pick a few thousand buttons as soon as it was light enough to see, and be gone soon after daylight."

"Hell, yes," I agreed, "I know it would work."

"Let's do it," he said. "It's Saturday morning. We could go down there today, pick tonight, and be back by noon tomorrow."

I went cold. So far it had all been theoretical. But now Jim was talking about really going back to that same town where the cops had promised to kill me if they ever saw me again. If they got their hands on me again, I knew it wouldn't be a week in a nice pleasant jail. I couldn't play the innocent college kid or pretend I didn't know what I was getting into. They'd either kill me on the spot, or send me to Parchman Farm, the infamous Texas State Penitentiary, for a long, long time.

I'd been in plenty of risky situations before and taken a lot of chances, but always I felt I was playing against the fairly slight odds of getting caught. Never had I done anything so completely and obviously dangerous, even demonstrably foolish. But if it worked, Jim and I could split ten grand for a few hours of being scared shitless. Working out the numbers, I figured that five thousand dollars would bring my life savings up to just about exactly five thousand dollars. What a difference that would make. I could buy a car instead of having to hitchhike everywhere. I could buy good expensive drugs.

But I think what decided me was the thought of actually getting my hands on enough peyote to be able to take as much as I wanted. Peyote always gave me the feeling that I was on the edge of some kind of breakthrough, some curtain through which I could just sense some other world. If I had enough, I could do it every day for a while; really see where the trip would take me; maybe pass through that curtain.

"Yeah, okay," I said. "Why not?" Jim grinned, but I could tell he was scared, too.

The first thing to do was to clean me up a bit. Jim already looked like your normal white-collar Texas guy. I couldn't quite go that route, but we thought I might be able to pass for a cowboy. We pulled my hair up on the top of my head and Bev shaved my hair up from my neck and ears. When I put on an old cowboy hat Joe found, I looked like a scruffy, bearded ranch hand — as long as I kept the hat on, that is.

Jim had a little red sports car, the first Datsun I had ever seen. With its twin seats and a tiny streamlined body with racing stripes, it looked like anything but a smuggler's vehicle. The down side was that the trunk was tiny. It wouldn't hold much more than a small gym bag. But Jim and Bev had a big steamer trunk in the attic of the garage. We lugged it down and cleaned it up so it looked respectable. We found some good strong straps and lashed it down tight on the luggage rack on the trunk lid. In the end it looked like the car in the Route 66 TV show. We decided that was a good look. If stopped, Jim could say he was off on a short vacation to Mexico. Since we didn't match, we could say I was a hitchhiker he'd picked up, on my way to the Rio Grande valley to look for work on a ranch. It just might work.

"It would not work!" said Elissa as soon as she heard of the plan. "Are you crazy, Brian? I can't believe you're even considering going back down there. Do you remember that night out in the desert; the guys with guns and clubs? They told us they'd kill us if they ever saw us again. Don't tell me you've forgotten that!"

I knew she was being sensible, but I was in no mood to be sensible. Sometimes I get these things rolling and I just want to see where they go, even though I'm perfectly aware it's not a good idea. Elissa was terrified by the very idea of going back to the river, and she begged and pleaded with me not to go. A funny thing happened to me. Even though I knew she was right and I shouldn't go, I didn't want to hear that. I wanted to go down there, get it done, and be done with it. I think part of it was to face my fear, to purge that pure, raw, loose-bowelled terror I'd felt that night. Those guys had threatened and ogled and terrorized Elissa, too, and I'd been helpless to protect her. In spite of my peaceable hippie ideals, I had enough testosterone in me to resent being humiliated like that, and this was a way of sticking it back in their faces. If I went back down there after all their threats and pulled it off, I'd be proving — to myself, at least — that they hadn't beaten me.

Elissa, of course, didn't understand any of that and thought I was just being stupid. She shouted and nagged at me for hours and I became angry and resentful. Finally I told her that I was going anyway. I think we both knew that something had broken between us.

Jim and I took off a few hours later. We had a great drive down, driving fast, smoking dope and talking and listening to country music on the radio. I told Jim that we'd heard a legend that the Navajo always eat the first button they find right away. To skip the ritual invites bad luck. Perhaps that's why Mike and I had been busted. Jim thought that sounded like a bullshit superstition.

I'd thought to look for the overpass where I'd almost frozen to death, but realized later that I hadn't even noticed it. I guess we were talking. It was just another invisible overpass like a thousand others.

We got down into Starr County on schedule just after dark. We kept well away from the town and any lights. We found a roadside pullout and parked the car. We wrapped up in sleeping bags and dozed off and on. At three AM we pulled out and continued towards Roma. I pointed out the dirt road, but we drove on by, went another mile, and pulled over and stopped the engine. Not a light; not a sound. Leaving the lights off, Jim swung around and we went back to the dirt road. There was a half moon out, so it wasn't completely dark. Jim drove slowly because the road was bad and the car was not built for off-road travel. We bounced and jounced along, occasionally scraping the muffler, until we came to the little wooden gate I remembered. Jim turned the car around and parked it behind a big juniper bush. I put a couple of tumbleweeds in front of it, and it was nearly invisible.

Grabbing the stack of old pillowcases we'd brought for bags, we climbed over the gate and started up the hill beyond. My ears were straining to catch any sound. I knew the Border Patrol must be out here somewhere, but I guessed they'd be down closer to the river, where the hills fall away to the valley. They'd be able to look down and see anybody crossing the river. Mike and I had first been spotted by a plane, and they could only do that in daylight. By that time, Jim and I planned to be long gone.

We climbed the first two ridges, and I pointed out the row of skeletal power lines marching over the next hill. Jim nodded. We hadn't spoken since we left the car, and I wondered what he was feeling. This was all new to him, and I was impressed that he'd come this far. He had courage, that was sure.

When we reached the bottom of the next valley, we left the dirt road and moved slowly through the sparse chaparral, bending low to peer under the larger bushes. Then I spotted my first button, lying right there in the moonlight. I caught Jim's arm and pointed. He squatted down to peer closely at it. He'd never seen peyote. It was a nice fat one, three or four inches across. I took out my knife and laid it flat on the ground next to the button, then sliced it off right at ground level. I picked it up and cored out the prickles from the middle and shaved off the little tufts of tiny thorns that dotted its surface. I rinsed off the last hairs with a splash from my water bottle. We looked at each other, and Jim nodded. I sliced it into four quarters and handed two to Jim. I popped one in my mouth and started to chew. Jim examined his for a moment, then followed suit.

It really is astounding how unbelievably bad peyote tastes. Every time I brace myself for the taste, and every time I'm surprised. I chewed it to a pulp and swallowed it with some difficulty. I looked over at Jim, squatting on his haunches under the bush. He had a rather stricken look on his face, but he was chewing gamely. When he saw me swallow, he did the same.

"Shit," he whispered.

"Much like it, yes," I agreed, popping the other quarter into my mouth.

When we had finished the button and washed the taste from our mouths, we spread out and started duck walking up the hill. Soon there were more buttons, then more, until we were almost walking on a pavement of buttons. Occasionally I heard a breathed "Wow!" from Jim when he came upon a particularly big one. In twenty minutes we had filled our first pillowcases. We tied them closed and stashed them under a bush, then started on the next. By the end of an hour, we had each filled three. I stood up to stretch my legs. Looking around, I realized I could see much farther that when we'd started.

"It's starting to get light," I whispered. "Want to try for some more?"

"No, let's not get stupid. We've got a shit load already."

"Right, let's get the fuck out of here." We tied up the bags and started back. By the time we got back to the car we each had heavy loads on our backs and it was definitely getting lighter. We opened the steamer trunk and stuffed in the full pillowcases. We had to mash them in to get the trunk latched again. We double-checked the lashing on the trunk, and then I hauled the tumbleweeds aside while Jim started the car. I jumped in and we started rolling quietly back down the hill.

With the car loaded, it scraped its bottom more, and we both winced at the noise every time it happened. I had images of us getting high-centered on one of these ruts and getting stuck. But we reached the highway without incident. I got out and peered up and down the road, then signaled to Jim and he pulled out onto the pavement. I hopped in, and we were off, heading north. After a half mile, Jim flipped on the lights and floored it.

I looked over at him. His face, lit from below by the dash lights, was shiny with sweat. His eyes were wild and his hair was blowing in the warm night wind. He looked over at me and grinned. I realized he was loving every minute of the adventure. Suddenly I was too. I also realized for the first time that we were totally ripped on the peyote. Nothing like getting it fresh.

Now all we had to worry about was the occasional Border Patrol checkpoints. It's hard to get out of the Rio Grande Valley without going through one, but they're only looking for illegal immigrants, and we didn't think they'd make us open the trunk. It was clearly too small to hide anybody in.

As it turned out, we didn't hit any checkpoints. We sailed back at about ninety-five miles an hour, whizzing across the flat Texas plains as fast as we could go. In late afternoon, we pulled into the driveway on McCart Street. The family poured out of the house to greet us. Elissa came out and hugged me and told me how glad she was to see me alive. It took three of us to carry the trunk into the kitchen. We set it on the floor and threw back the lid. A rank and indescribable odor emerged. The pillowcases were soaked through with dark green juice. We dumped them out on the kitchen table. The buttons bumped and rolled across the cracked Formica. A dozen or so rolled off the edge and thudded soggily on the floor. With the last bag emptied, the pile covered the entire table and rose to a peak at least eighteen inches high. We all sat and stared at it in wonder.

"That, my friends," said Joe, "is one fuck of a lot of peyote."

Chapter Twenty-One
We're Cooking Now

We cleaned a few dozen buttons and passed them out. Not to be left behind, Jim and I each ate another. Soon everybody looked a little green. There were the usual comments about the taste and texture. When fresh, they're about like boiled potatoes — firm, but easily bitten or mashed, slightly slimy, and about the color of a dark avocado. A few hours after being cut, however, they start to soften up and they get covered in mucous, like okra. After two or three days they become wet and flaccid like a rotten potato, and turn a bilious green somewhere between army green and stewed-pea green. They ooze and get covered in something very like snot. At no time do they taste good, but when they're going off they do not improve.

But for now they were as appetizing as they were going to get, so we dug into them with a will. There were twenty or thirty people tripping non-stop the rest of that day, all night, and the whole next day. I was finally able to really take all I wanted and could handle, and I had an absolutely great time.

By Sunday night, a few of us were seated again around the kitchen table, staring rather blearily at a pile of peyote that was but little diminished and obviously heading south fast. It was clear there was no way we could possibly eat even a major portion of them before they were rotten and inedible. It seemed a terrible waste. We could put a few handfuls in the freezer, but we didn't know if they'd be edible when thawed. Someone suggested canning them in mason jars, but Bev said they were already too far gone and it would be an immense amount of work.

"How about cooking them?" Joe suggested. "We could make a stew or something."

"Ew," said Elissa. "Peyote stew? Yuk."

"We could cook it down into a smaller quantity and bottle it," Jim offered.

"That might work," I said. "Maybe it would be like a milk shake."

"You know," said Joe, "that's not a bad idea. If it were concentrated, we wouldn't have to eat so much of it. And I think it would be easier to drink it than to chew up those slimy buttons."

"Yeah," said several people. "You could just hold your nose and gulp down a big mug of it. Touching them and smelling them is the worst."

"If we really boiled it down," said Bev, "we could make it really concentrated so you'd only have to drink a little bit."

"Hey, that would be great," I enthused. "That would be easy. Maybe we wouldn't even get sick. But how could we cook it down that much? With this much you'd have to boil it for days."

"How about a pressure cooker?" asked Jim.

"It'd have to be a big one," said Elissa, "or we'd be cooking five hundred batches."

Joe snapped his fingers. "I know a guy who works in a restaurant. I bet he could borrow one of those big industrial cookers. That wouldn't take so long."

"Wow, do you think we could get one?" asked Bev.

"I can ask." He went to the phone and called a guy. When he returned a few minutes later, he was smiling. "He said they have a couple of cookers and there's one they haven't used in months. It's old, but he says it stills works."

"Can he get it for us?"

"Yeah. He's going to liberate it after his shift tonight and bring it over tomorrow."

"Outasight, Joe," we all exclaimed. "Way to go, brother!"

We passed a number or two to ease the coming down off the trip. People started to fade toward bed, and for once I wasn't one of the last to crash. It had been a big weekend.

Joe's friend brought the pressure cooker over in the morning. It was a big heavy cast iron thing with a massive two-handled lid with a huge pressure gauge and relief valve sticking up from the top. He said to fill it up with whatever we wanted to cook, cover it with water, and keep it over a steady fire for as long as necessary. Since we didn't mention what we were cooking, we didn't have any way of guessing how long it was going to take. We rinsed it out with boiling water and got started right away. Three of us sat around the table, taking a button, coring it, shaving the stickers off, rinsing it in cold water, and cutting it into bite-size chunks. When we had filled a big mixing bowl, we dumped it into the pot. Since we were starting with the rottenest buttons first, it was not a pleasant job. Soon we were covered with the viscous green gunk and the kitchen was slippery with it. Finally the pot was full. We'd used maybe half of the peyote. We covered the buttons with boiling water; two or three gallons at least, then put the lid on and sealed it down. We put it on the stove and turned the burners up to full. Then we cleaned up the mess we'd made and took showers.

We cooked the pot the rest of that day. There were interminable debates about how long we should cook it. After a few hours, some of us wanted to open it up and take a look; others didn't want to waste the heat and pressure we already had. When Jim and Bev got home from work, they commented on how rank the kitchen smelled. With the pile of buttons reeking in a garbage can and the steam from the cooker, it was like living inside a peyote button. We ate some more buttons and tripped most of the night away.

Sometime during the night we couldn't stand it anymore and turned the burner off. We waited a little while, and then released the pressure. A huge blast of rancid-smelling steam hissed out, causing quite a barrage of complaints. Then two guys held the pot with towels while two of us took off the lid and set it aside. We all peered in. The quantity was considerably reduced. The pot was less than half full of a thick green liquid, rather like split pea soup. I got a slotted spoon and lifted out some buttons. They were shrunken, half-digested lumps, and pure white. We rinsed one off, let it cool, and then examined it. It was hard, like a raw potato. I sliced off a tiny slice and gingerly tasted it. Everyone watched me curiously.

"Doesn't taste like anything," I shrugged. "Can't even smell it."

"Hey, I bet that means we got everything out of it," said Joe. "We got all the color and smell out, so I guess we got all the mescaline out, too. It's all in the stew. We peered at the soup with some respect.

"What now?" I asked.

"I think we should dip out the buttons and throw them away," said Bev. "Then cut up the rest and throw them in and cook it some more. That way all the goodies will be in the one batch."

"Yeah," I said. "We'll cook them all up together and make one super-concentrated stew." We got to work and cleaned and cut up the rest of the buttons. There were still too many for the pot, so we filled it with water again, closed it up, and got it cooking again. Then we went to bed.

In the morning we woke to a terrible smell of peyote throughout the house. Everything seemed to be all right, but the smell from the steam was filling the house. We opened the pot and threw in the remaining buttons, then started it up again. I slept most of the day, worn out from four heavy trips in three days. In the late afternoon, the smell woke me up. I wandered out to the kitchen to check it out. The entire pot was black from staying on the burner for forty-eight hours. Steam was still hissing from the valve. I felt light-headed, whether from the tripping or the smell, I couldn't tell.

Most of the others had gone out to get away from the smell. Elissa and I decided to take a walk as well. As we walked away from the house, Elissa sniffed the air.

"Is it just me, or can I still smell that shit?" she asked.

"I don't know," I replied. "My nose is so full of peyote stink I can't smell anything else."

We walked around a few blocks and soon felt much better. As we came down the alley behind the house, we looked at each other. There was no mistaking the rank jungle reek of peyote, thick in the air. Two neighbors were talking over the common fence.

"Well, I don't know either, Marge," said one. "It's like to drive Jim Bob crazy."

"Oh, I know," replied the other. "My Hal is down checking all the plumbing. He can't tell where it's coming from, either."

"I've called the city sanitation. They're going to send a truck to investigate. I think it's backed up somewhere."

They saw us walking by and gave us that fish-eyed stare all the locals had when trying not to see there were hippies in the neighborhood. We hurried home. Jim and Bev had just gotten home.

"Christ almighty," said Jim. "The whole neighborhood stinks! I could smell it in the car when I turned onto the street."

"It's awful," said Bev, covering her nose with a dishtowel. She looked at the rest of us.

"Look, I think I've been pretty damn accommodating about this whole chemistry experiment. But I want my house back. We've got to get rid of that awful stuff."

"We just heard some of the neighbors talking," said Elissa. "They've called the sanitation department to come out and find where the smell's coming from."

"That's no good," I said. "What can we do?"

"Turn it off, for a start," said Bev, turning off the burner. "And open the windows. I'm getting a headache." We released the pressure, enduring one final blast of foul steam. We opened it up and let it cool a bit, then strained out the last of the buttons. When it had cooled, we poured it out into a juice pitcher. It made about two quarts of a thick dark green juice. We hauled the remains out to the back yard and buried it, then cleaned up. We took the pot out to Joe's car to return to his friend. It occurred to me that he might not be entirely pleased at the condition of the cooker. I resolved not to eat at his friend's restaurant. Then we sat for a while staring at the pitcher of peyote juice.

"You know," I mused, "I figure there's at least four hundred buttons that went into that pot, some of them really big. If all that mescaline is still in the juice, that's four hundred pretty good trips, or a couple of hundred ripsnortin' wall bangers."

"Yuh," Joe agreed. "That's a lot of trips, even for this family."

"It's also worth a lot of money," I pointed out.

"How could we sell it now?" Joe replied. "Put it in coke bottles?"

"No, man. A whole trip's worth is about a half a teaspoonful of the stuff. We'd have to sell it in little tiny bottles."

"Medicine droppers?" somebody suggested.

"I guess we could just let people take a swig."

"A very small swig. If you drank very much of this stuff, they'd never find where your head landed."

"The only way I could think of would be to give 'em a straw," said Jim. "Let 'em start to take a toke, then whip it out of their mouth."

We all laughed at the image. "It might work, though," I said.

"You might get punched out, too."

"So we invite four hundred heads over here to have a snort off my juice pitcher?" asked Bev. "I don't think so."

"No, we should take it somewhere where there are lots of heads around," I said. "Then we could just hawk it on the street and get rid of it fast."

"Where could we do that?" asked Joe. "Want to try the Botanical Gardens again?"

"Perhaps not," I agreed. "Where is the nearest concentration of hippies? Someplace with a busy street scene."

"There's quite a few hippies in Dallas, I guess," said Bev. "But there's no street scene at all. It's just a few clubs."

"Houston is supposed to have a good scene," suggested Joe. "I heard that there's lots of people that hang out someplace called Allen's Landing."

"Yeah, that might work," I said. "How far is Houston?"

"Four or five hours south and east," said Jim.

"Up for another drive this weekend, brother?" I asked.

Jim smiled. "Sure, why not?"

Chapter Twenty-Two
Houston

The next day several of us tried a sip of the juice to see how it was. It tasted unbearably vile, but we took such tiny sips we could rinse it down immediately, so it was really pretty easy to get down. We waited an hour or two, trying to decide if we needed to take more. Then we decided we didn't. Then we wondered if we'd taken too much. By the next morning we knew we had a truly great product. We kept a quart for ourselves and set the other jar aside for sale.

That Saturday morning Jim and Bev, Joe, Elissa, and I rode down to Houston in Joe's old car. When we got there we asked around till we found Allen's Landing. It was a newly redeveloped industrial area down by the Houston Ship Channel. We found a place to park a few blocks away around sunset. We had the juice in a glass one-quart orange juice bottle. We put a plastic straw in it. It was a little too long, but we just screwed on the top and bent the straw. I tucked the jar in the inner pocket of my pea jacket and we walked down to Allen's Landing.

It was an interesting scene. It was no Haight-Ashbury, but there were a surprising number of freaks around. There were a number of bars and music clubs and open areas to hang out. There was music playing and lots of people strolling and shopping and sitting around. We strolled from one end of the street to the other, studying the crowds, the traffic flow, and the general ambience. I noticed two or three small but fairly obvious drug transactions, mostly in the shadows under the trees out in the park. Two or three guys passed us, mumbling the usual hippie street mantra: "Grass, speed, acid?" It seemed a pretty good place to try out our scheme. We sat on a park bench and watched the crowd for a while. Then I accosted a stoned-looking young kid in bell-bottoms and a tie-dyed tee shirt.

"Wanna do some peyote, brother?" I asked. He looked at me in surprise. He wore two strands of beads and had his hair brushed down to his eyebrows like John Sebastian. I guess he thought he looked pretty cool. He looked us over cautiously.

"Well, maybe, I guess. I never tried it."

"You've done acid?"

"Yeah?"

"It's like that, only without that acid edge. No harsh colors; no speed nervousness. It's one hundred percent organic, brother. All natural."

"Where'd you get it?"

"Never you mind, my curious friend. All you need to know is that it's very, very good, and it will cost you a mere thin nickel."

"Only five bucks? For a peyote trip?" he exclaimed ingenuously, if unwisely. "Well, sure. Can I get two, so I can take it back to school? My roommate would love this."

"Ah, well, no. That wouldn't work."

"Huh? Why not?"

This was the tricky part of my sales spiel. "Um, it doesn't work as a takeout item. It's in liquid form, you see. Strictly one per customer. It must be consumed on the premises."

"What? Liquid? I thought peyote was a cactus."

"It is. It was. But my associates and I have processed it; rendered it, so to speak, into a more convenient and palatable form. We distilled it down to its pure essence, so you receive all the potency and beneficial effects, without the less enjoyable aspects of eating the cactus."

"So I'd have to eat it…"

"Drink it."

"… whatever, right now?"

"Yes."

"How?"

"It's a simple enough proposition. You give me five dollars. I have a bottle and a straw. You take a sip — a very small one. Very soon you feel very good."

He stared at me for a minute. "How long does it last?"

"Six, maybe eight hours."

"Wow. Well, okay." He took out five dollars and palmed it to me. At least he knew enough to not wave it around.

"Walk this way." I led him around behind a hedge where it was dark. I took out the bottle and opened it. The straw popped up.

"This juice is very concentrated," I warned him. "This jar contains around four hundred trips, so a little dab'll do ya. Also, be prepared. We're still, ah, working on the taste."

"Okay." He reached for the jar. I pulled it back.

"No, I'll hold it. You just take a sip."

"Shit. Okay." He leaned forward and took the straw in his mouth. I watched the liquid go up the straw. As soon as it passed his lips, I pulled the straw away.

"Hey, come on," he complained. "I hardly got any." Then a surprised look came over his face. "Jesus God. What is that shit?" He made a face like his shorts were too tight. "Christ, did you poison me?"

"Trust me, my friend," I said. "I'll be around here all night. Your stomach may feel a bit unsettled in an hour or so, but ride with it. By nine o'clock you'll be dancing with the angels."

"I don't know," he said. "I didn't get hardly any."

"Look. Come back here in three hours. If you want some more, I'll be here."

"Well, okay, I guess." He wandered off and was soon lost in the crowd. I went back and sat down with the others.

"One down, three hundred and ninety-nine to go."

Bev complimented me on my sales style. I shrugged it off. "Just doing my job, ma'am. It's all in a day's work."

So that's what we did for the next few hours. We took turns selling, and frequently moved to avoid drawing a crowd. Business was fairly steady, and the level of liquid gradually went down. We all had our pockets stuffed full of five-dollar bills. By nine or ten the word had clearly gotten around because people started coming up to us asking for sips.

At one point I found myself in a circle of five or six fairly drunk college kids, all of them asking me dumb questions and spending too much time talking and not enough buying. I kept scanning the crowd around us, watching for any suspicious signs we were under surveillance. I noticed a kid with a huge grin on his face watching the operation. I recognized my first customer.

"Hey, bro," I called to him. "You're back. You like another hit?"

The other kids turned to look at him. He grinned like the sun, a relaxed, mellow look on his face.

"Another hit?" he said, and then he started to laugh. "No, I don't think I will. In fact, I don't think I'm going to need another hit for a good long time. Man, this is the best trip I ever had."

Perfect timing. "There you have it, folks," I said. "Another satisfied customer." I sold eight hits in one round.

And so it went, hour after hour. Soon it seemed that everybody I talked to was already tripping on our peyote. You could spot the ones who hadn't come on yet. They were making faces and spitting and trying to get the taste out of their mouths. Many ordered cokes or something else to kill the taste. I'll bet that was a great night for the soft drink vendors. They must have wondered what hit them.

The ones who had already come on were blissful. Looking out across the park, I could see dozens of groups of people just sitting and looking around, gazing up at the stars, or strolling beside the ship channel. All I could see were grins in the dark.

By two o'clock the crowd was thinning out and sales dropped off. We just had a few sips left, so we all topped off our highs and walked back to the car. It had been a memorable evening. I suspect it was long remembered by Houston, as well. Relaxed now, rich and happy, we started the long drive back to Fort Worth, and into drug legend.

Chapter Twenty-Three
The Crawford Decision

Back home, we continued our routine of partying while we waited for my case to come up. Finally the date of my indictment arrived and I got as cleaned up as I could and went downtown to the courthouse. My attorneys were afraid they would throw in some extra charges, or worse yet, drop the vagrancy charge, but I was finally formally indicted on vagrancy and loitering, both misdemeanors punishable by up to thirty days in county jail. I entered a plea of not guilty. My bail was renewed, and I went home.

The peyote adventure had done nothing to lessen my fame in our circle of friends. More and more people kept coming over to the house to get stoned and try some of the famous peyote parfait. Lots of these new people were sexy young college girls from Tarrant County Junior College. I was particularly struck by one dark-haired cutie named Sukey, a name I had never encountered before except on mules.

One hot sunny day a bunch of us, stoned as usual, got out a ladder and climbed up on the roof of the house. The house was basically C-shaped with the open side toward the garage, so although the neighbors could see the ladder, once on the roof we were completely unseen. The house was in the middle of a huge tract of similar one-story houses, so no one could look down at us. The only thing visible from the roof was an immense high-tension tower next door, known to the family as the Flower Power Power Tower.

So we climbed up on the roof to smoke and sunbathe. Some of the girls took their tops off, including Sukey, which really turned me on. Several of us took everything off and spent the afternoon dozing and smoking and having a great time. I was fascinated by Sukey's nude body, and developed a strong desire for her. Having Elissa just downstairs frustrated me. As open and free as sex was at the house, it would not do to fuck Sukey with Elissa right there. My frustration triggered a mean streak in me. We were laughing and teasing and flirting, and suddenly I grabbed all of Sukey's clothes and climbed down from the roof. She was freaked out and begged me to give her clothes back, but I wouldn't for a long time. Something about having her up there, naked and helpless, really turned me on. It's the only time I ever remember intentionally being cruel to anyone I liked, and it has stuck with me ever since. After a while Martha took her clothes up to her and Sukey got dressed and left without speaking to me. Who could blame her? Elissa heard about it, of course, and was not amused.

Elissa sensed that we were drifting apart and became anxious about it. I think she still really loved me and wanted us to stay together. But I just kept being distracted by all the other women around and couldn't give her the attention she needed. I simply didn't have any interest in a committed relationship, and certainly not an exclusive one. She couldn't handle that. It wasn't fun for either of us.

There was another young couple, James and Muriel, that started coming around more often. They both looked pretty straight, but they liked to party, too. Muriel was quite attractive and I thought I sensed her eye on me, but they seemed to be pretty tight together. James was rather intellectual and interesting to talk to. He and Jim and I had a lot of good talks together. Joe and Martha became a couple and seemed to be happy.

Finally in June, my case at last came to trial. The attorney from the ACLU met me in the hallway outside the courtroom. He told me to answer any questions honestly, be polite, and not try to make any speeches. He'd handle it all. That was fine with me.

Then we went in and sat down in the audience. There was already a trial going on. A young tough-looking guy about my age was up for auto theft. He'd lifted a Mustang and gone joyriding. His lawyer didn't put up much of a defense, and no one seemed to care what happened either way, including the judge, the attorneys, or even the accused. He was posing and preening for the girls in the court, I guess thinking he was pretty cool. Then the judge told him to stand up.

"Young man, I find your excuses to be completely without merit," said the judge, looking at him severely over the top of his glasses. "You got drunk, stole a car, and drove around recklessly, endangering your own life, and more importantly, those of law-abiding citizens. I find you guilty of grand larceny, auto, and sentence you to seven years in the state penitentiary." He banged his gavel. "Next case!"

The guy stood there looking stunned. I don't know what he expected, but it sure wasn't seven years. His face went beet red.

"That's bullshit!" he shouted at the judge. "Seven years? That's nothing! Hell, I can do seven years sitting on the can!"

The judge looked at him, no sign of annoyance on his face. "Is that so?" He jotted down a note, and then looked up. "Well, in that case I'll give you two more years to wipe your ass. Next case."

The guy looked like he was going to explode, but a beefy bailiff came and took him out. The courtroom was quiet. I did some math. Let's see, he would have gotten out in '75, but that smart remark made it 1977 before he walked. I imagined that those last two years would be very long. I learned something about the absolute power of a judge. I resolved to be as polite and contrite as I knew how.

The court clerk stood up.

"City of Fort Worth versus Brian Kenneth Crawford, your honor. Vagrancy and loitering."

"Mr. Crawford?" said the judge. "Please come forward."

I got up and went through the gate and stood in front of the bench. The judge looked me over.

"Have you an attorney, Mr. Crawford? If not, one will be assigned from the public defender's office."

My attorney stood up. "I represent Mr. Crawford, you honor. William Johnson." There was an immediate buzz of whispers around the room. I saw the district attorneys look at each other.

"I see." The judge looked from him to me, made a note, and then glanced over the case. "And do you still plead not guilty, Mr. Crawford?"

"I do, you honor," I replied.

"Well, let's get started then. I see the arrest was made by Patrolman Gutierrez. Is he in court today?"

A uniformed cop stood up. "I am, your honor." I glanced at him in surprise. He was a Latino, but the cops who'd grabbed me were all white. I wasn't sure if I'd recognize them, but I knew this guy wasn't one of them. I glanced over at my attorney. He met my eye and gestured to me to remain silent.

"Would you please come up and tell us what you observed on..." he glanced down again, "...on Sunday, March 31, 1968? You may sit down there, Mr. Crawford." I sat down as the cop took the stand. He took out a small notebook and leafed through it. He started to read.

"I was on patrol in the Botanical Gardens that day. I observed a group of young people in the fountains."

"*In* the fountains, did you say?" interrupted the judge.

"Yes, your honor."

"What were they doing there?"

"Well, I guess sort of dancing around and splashing in the water, your honor."

I leaned over to my attorney. "I was never anywhere near the fountains," I whispered.

"Doesn't matter," he replied.

"What else did you observe, Officer?"

"Well, there were lots of people on the grass, and walking around and so on."

"It is a public park, is it not, Officer Gutierrez?"

"Uh, yes, it is, your honor. But these people were making a real disturbance."

"What sort of disturbance?"

"They were being very disorderly, your honor. You know, shouting and all."

The judge looked over his glasses at the cop. "Do you mean shouting out political slogans, obscenities, epithets, threats against the government, incitements to riot?"

"Well, no. But they were shouting, and laughing, like. Loudly."

"Laughing with criminal intent," observed the judge dryly. He made another note. "I see. And what did you observe Mr. Crawford doing at this time?"

The cop studied his notebook again. "He was part of a group that was obstructing the sidewalk, your honor."

"That's bullshit," I hissed to my lawyer. "I was on the grass under a tree."

"Doesn't matter," he replied again.

"These people were making a disturbance," continued the cop. "They were lying on the sidewalk and frightening people trying to use the park. Some of them were urinating in the reflecting pool."

"He's lying," I whispered again. "Nobody did that, certainly not me."

He waved me aside airily. "Doesn't matter." I was starting to get concerned about him. Why wasn't he objecting to all these accusations? The cop was lying. Maybe he hadn't even been there that day. He could accuse me of anything and it was just the word of a homeless drifter against one of Fort Worth's finest.

"Anything else, Officer?" asked the judge.

Gutierrez paged hurriedly through his notebook. "Uh, yes, your honor. Uh, here it is." He started reading again. "I saw the accused taking drugs and engaging in lewd behavior, and accosting citizens trying to go about their business. That is all, your honor."

The judge looked at my lawyer. "Cross-examine, counselor?"

Mr. Johnson stood up. "Officer Gutierrez," he began. "Let me get this straight. You personally saw Mr. Crawford urinating in the reflecting pool?"

"Yes, sir, I did." I started waving and gesturing angrily, but Johnson waved me to keep still.

"And you saw Mr. Crawford obstructing a sidewalk, engaging in lewd behavior, taking drugs, and accosting citizens, is that correct?"

"Yes, sir, I did," replied Gutierrez with a defiant tone.

"Then, Officer Gutierrez, I wonder why you didn't charge Mr. Crawford with any of those acts?"

"Uh, what?"

The judge interrupted. "Why didn't your department charge him with any of that? The charges are vagrancy and loitering. There is no mention in the indictment of any public disturbance or lewd behavior."

Of course, I realized. All those trumped-up accusations had nothing to do with vagrancy and loitering.

"So how did you determine that Mr. Crawford was loitering?"

"Uh, well, I just saw him doing it, your honor."

"He was loitering? You observed him loitering?"

"Yes, sir, your honor."

"So he was in fact not doing anything at the time you observed him. Isn't that what loitering implies?"

"Yes, your honor, that is correct."

"If I may submit, your honor," said Johnson. "The city builds public parks for the purpose of loitering."

The judge looked at both of them. "Hmmm." Clearly he was not pleased with the way this was going.

"Now," he went on. "As to the second charge of vagrancy. How did you determine that Mr. Crawford was vagrant?"

"Oh, I could tell just by looking at him, your honor."

The judge glared at him. "Oh, you could, could you? So you observed that Mr. Crawford did not have ten dollars on him? From what distance?"

"Oh, well, I... well, he looked like a vagrant. I mean, he didn't have a shirt on."

"Yes, I see. Most damning. And when did you determine that Mr. Crawford didn't have any money?"

"Well, when we got him down to the station, I guess."

"So at the time of the arrest you didn't know if he had any money? In fact, he could have a thousand dollar bill in his wallet."

"Uh, he didn't look like he did, your honor. He looked like he was broke."

"Apparently that was not the case, was it? Mr. Crawford has in fact hired a private attorney. You can't do that if you're broke."

"Uh, just to set the record straight, your honor," said Johnson, "I am defending Mr. Crawford pro bono."

"You are?" asked the judge in surprise. "May I ask why?"

"You may, your honor. I work with the American Civil Liberties Union and we are..."

The judge banged his gavel down loud, startling all of us. "Case dismissed. All charges are dropped. You are free to go, Mr. Crawford. And Officer Gutierrez, I don't want to see you ever bring me another case so utterly without merit." He stood up angrily.

"All rise," shouted the clerk, and we all stood as the judge swept out of the courtroom.

"Wow," I said. "That was incredible. You destroyed that cop."

Johnson was putting his papers back in his briefcase. "We lost, Mr. Crawford. We lost again."

"Oh, yeah, that's right. I forgot. Sorry. I guess."

"It's worth the effort. All we can do is keep trying."

"Well, thanks, Mr. Johnson. Thanks a lot."

We shook hands and I walked out of court. I was only slightly disappointed about the landmark Crawford Decision. I was finally free of legal hassles again.

Chapter Twenty-Four
On the Road Again

The parties continued on McCart Street. Elissa and I were pretty much on separate paths now. There was talk of her continuing to California in July with Jim and Bev and a bunch of the family. I felt that I'd pretty much finished with Fort Worth and was hot to get on out of town. I made more of an effort to line up a ride west. A week or so later somebody I didn't know contacted me and told me he knew about two guys who were driving to LA soon. I made the connection and called the guys up.

They sounded pretty messed up on the phone. They wanted to go to LA to go surfing. They had a truck. They just needed some money. I told them I could pay a third of the gas and help drive. They said that would be okay, but they only had room for one. I agreed, and we arranged that they would come pick me up on their way out of town a couple of days from now.

When I told Elissa I'd gotten a ride for one, she really flipped out. She started crying and saying that I was abandoning her out here in the wilds of Texas. I knew she wasn't happy about my leaving without her, but I was surprised by the level of her anger and hurt. I hadn't seen it as my abandoning her. We'd just been traveling together, and now we were going on our own. I thought that she felt that she was among friends there with the McCart family. They all certainly liked her and assured her that she was welcome to stay there as long as she liked. I figured she could stay on with them if she liked, or she could go wherever she wanted to next. But she accused me of luring her from home with unspoken promises, and then just dumping her on the road. There didn't seem to be anything I could say to that, but I had no intention of keeping the relationship going just on that basis. I just wanted to move on. It made for a sad ending to a nice time together, and I felt guilty for hurting her.

Two days later, my ride showed up. It was two longhaired cowboys in a rusty old faded red Ford pickup truck. They were towing a beat-up Airstream trailer, one of those globular silver things. A surfboard stuck out of the back of the pickup, amidst a pile of duffel bags, garbage bags, and sleeping bags. The guys seemed really wasted and were barely coherent when I was trying to nail down the arrangements. I agreed to a third of the gas and any driving they wanted me to do. Both of them seemed unable to sit still and kept scratching and twitching like they were really uncomfortable. I didn't get a good feeling from them at all. They had big circles under their eyes and had a kind of dull, pasty, unhealthy look. I could see they were junkies and really wasted. I'd never heard of junkie surfers before. But it was the only ride that had come up in a couple of months. Also the unpleasant scene with Elissa made me want to get out of town in a hurry.

I said goodbye to the family with lots of hugs and kisses and promises to keep in touch. They all expected to be in San Francisco in a few months and we said we'd meet up in Haight-Ashbury. When I went to say goodbye to Elissa, she really broke down. She cried and begged me not to go. But I was even more determined to get out of what had turned into a very unhealthy relationship. I unwrapped her arms and walked out, leaving her crying. I felt like shit. This wasn't how it was supposed to end.

I climbed in the cab of the truck with the two weird dudes, and we pulled away from the house. I waved to the family that was watching, and then they were gone. We rolled through the outskirts of Fort Worth, and then got on the freeway, heading west. I was on the road again.

Acknowledgements

I first published this story on the Internet in the early 1990's. Some years later, I received an e-mail from Rick Benedict who had stumbled across the story. He remembered those times well, especially the big bust in the Botanical Gardens. "I was there that day," he said, and what's more, he had pictures to prove it. He sent me the pictures I've included on pages 118 and 119, including the last one, which he labeled "a longhair none of us knew." It turns out to be the only picture of me from that era. I added the pictures to the online story.

The coincidence continued a few years later when I received an e-mail from Alyse Dar, who had also come across the story online. She too had been in the park that day, and was astonished to see a picture of herself in the story (the girl in the middle in the flowered shirt).

Thanks to Rick and Alyse for taking the trouble to contact me, and for keeping alive the memory of the wonderful community of hippies in Fort Worth.